WHEN A MAN EXHALES

A Memoir From the Brother of Marvin Gaye

Antwaun Gay

When a Man Exhales: A Memoir from the Brother of Marvin Gaye
Copyright ©2024 Antwaun Gay.

ISBN: 979-8-218-43161-7

All rights reserved. No part of this book may be reproduced or used in any manner without written permission of the copyright owner except for the use of quotations in a book review.

BIBLE PERMISSIONS
Scripture taken from the New King James Version®. Copyright© 1982 by Thomas Nelson. Used by permission. All rights reserved.

Scripture taken from the King James Version is public domain in the United States. The King James Version, 1987 printing.

ALL RIGHTS RESERVED. No part of this Book may be reproduced or transmitted in any form whatsoever, electronic, or mechanical, including photocopying, recording, or by any informational storage or retrieval system without express written, dated, and signed permission from the author.

Find out more by visiting AntwaunGay.com

Editorial Team
Danika Deva, Managing Editor - Be Intentional Ministries, DanikaDeva.com
Valerie Riese, Editor - Faithful Pen Content Services LLC, valerieriese.com
Niki Banning, Editor - NikiB Virtual Services, nikibvirtualservices.com
Kathy Gifford, Editing and Design - kathygifford.solutions.com
Cover Photo and Design by Annie Eggleston,
https://www.behance.net/anniewatsone?locale=en_US&

DEDICATION

To my mother, Sandra, and to my wife, Carolyn. Words cannot express how much both of you mean to me.

Mother,
From the day of my birth till now, you have covered me with your prayers. I know I have been kept and delivered from dangers seen and unseen. One of the most precious and vital things you have done for me on this earth has been to pray for me. You have loved and endured much, and I pray this dedication blesses your heart.

Carolyn,
There is no finer woman on earth than you! You have loved me through the best and worst of me. Through you, I see God's love, patience, and forgiveness towards me ever more clearly. Thank you for encouraging me to leave the past behind when guilt and self-condemnation tried to drown me. May God use you to help millions of women, and may He give us the grace to make our latter years greater than the former. You will always be My Morning Cup of Tea!

"Many daughters have done virtuously, But thou excellest them all. Favour is deceitful, and beauty is vain: But a woman that feareth the LORD, she shall be praised."
- Proverbs 31:29-30 (KJV)

Table of Contents

Acknowledgements		i
Introduction		vii
Chapter 1	Father... WHY?—Unspeakable Pain	1
Chapter 2	Misfit	9
Chapter 3	A Different World	13
Chapter 4	Pretty Little Country Girl	21
Chapter 5	Life Lessons	29
Chapter 6	Northumberland Young Baller	37
Chapter 7	The Rivalry	43
Chapter 8	The Coach	49
Chapter 9	The Return	59
Chapter 10	New Addition	63
Chapter 11	Bittersweet	67
Chapter 12	Club Life	71
Chapter 13	Why Me?	75
Chapter 14	Jesus Saves	81
Chapter 15	The Awakening	87
Chapter 16	Unequally Yoked	95
Chapter 17	Someone Will Live and Not Die	99
Chapter 18	Carolyn—Forever My Lady	107
Chapter 19	Growth and Reflection	111
Chapter 20	The Deadly Inception	115
Chapter 21	The Move	121
Chapter 22	The Coldest Encounter	123
Chapter 23	Lustful Games	133
Chapter 24	Standing in Silent Awe	139
Chapter 25	The Call	147
Chapter 26	The Mentor and the Storm	155
Chapter 27	The Storm	161
Chapter 28	Slip, Sliding Away	167
Chapter 29	Just like Family	169
Chapter 30	Prodigal Son	177
Chapter 31	Running Away	181
Chapter 32	Falling Deeper	187
Chapter 33	Stupid Minded	191
Chapter 34	She's Not Here	195
Chapter 35	Love Lifted Me	199
Bibliography		207

Acknowledgements

Many people have been a blessing to my family and me, no matter how long or short the season. I am truly grateful to God for the ways He has used each of you to help, support, and encourage me over and over. While I can't acknowledge everyone, please know I am genuinely thankful for all of you.

I want to thank the late Dr. John A. Cherry and Diana Cherry and Bishop John A. Cherry II and wife Reverend LaWanda Cherry for allowing God to use both of you to help me grow in wisdom and understanding. Special thanks to Dr. Cherry, who guided me in my early walk with the Lord. I'm also thankful for the late Frederick K. Price and Pastor Charles Stanley, who helped me tremendously in my early walk. I can never say that God didn't send pastors after HIS own heart to feed me with knowledge and understanding.

A special thanks to Pastor Keith and Minister Lynn Kearse, Rev. Lawrence and Janice Davies, Pastor James and Rev. Teresa Ransome, Pastor Terrence and Minister Kimberly Jennings, Pastor Brian and Angie Gullins, Pastor Mike Taylor, Pastor Leonard B. Lacey, Pastor Ricky Wilson and the late Pastor Connie Wilson, Pastor Scott and Danika Covington, all of whom God has placed lovingly in our lives. I have been blessed, encouraged, rebuked, and strengthened by your preaching, teaching, counsel, and, more importantly, your walk.

Apostle John H. Bibbens and Apostle Rohan Gordon, thank you for giving me the opportunity to work my gift for a season under your leadership. Much appreciation to Pastor Darryl Williams and Dr. Donna Rhaney and all the ministers, teachers, professors, and classmates from Alpha Bible College and Fredericksburg Bible Institute during my attendance.

With gratitude to my CURRENT leaders, Bishop Derek and Pastor Yeromitou Grier. I am thankful for your leadership and the timely messages which God preaches through you.

James Fletcher, Darryl Samuel, Cledith Lee, Kevin Fletcher, and Robert Beck, I thank God for your love and friendship. Michael Stevenson and Robert Bailey, your coaching and leadership have helped me pour into thousands of youth over the years. Thank you for your mentorship.

Arlene Council, Gilda Retta Taylor, Dr. Mary McGee, and Terry Schmohl. Thank you for being there for both of us, especially Carolyn, personally and spiritually, through the years.

Majorie Parrish Taylor, I am grateful for your love and support to us, our children, and grandchildren.

Richard and Shenita Mallard, I am thankful for your friendship and taking us in at a very important time in our lives.

Thank you, Shelly Bivins, for your support and love from day one. Your insight, guidance, and friendship have been a blessing. May God continue to connect us in the next chapter of this journey.

To A & U and the boys and RW and the boys. I am grateful for your love, support, and friendship; it has been a blessing. You are family and you know who you are.

Donna Kennedy, thank you for being a loving sister and prayer warrior.

Heartfelt gratitude to Mrs. Roseamary Balgavy for being a great teacher and helping me tremendously with your knowledge and wisdom in helping to polish my manuscript. I truly love you.

I am grateful for Danika Covington, Valerie Riese, and Niki Banning for your editorial expertise and help in bringing this book to fruition. Kathy Gifford, thank you for wrapping the book up in your phenomenal design work, and Annie, Eggelston, thank you for my fabulous cover.

Thank you, Pastor James Hayward, for the use of your studio and Wesley Rose for your fabulous videography.

A special thanks to Patricia Adams for being the one who not only pushed me to finish the book in the beginning, but who started the process while giving me my first interview. You gave of your time, resources, and care to help me share my story with the world. May God continue to bless you mightily for your sacrifice.

To Francine Elizebath Natal and Arsenia Snow, I am grateful for your help in the early stages of this book and your time, knowledge, and talent. Your sincere help and encouragement are not forgotten.

Pastor Scott Covington, I thank God for your friendship. You are my brother, and I am grateful for your selfless love to Carolyn, me, and countless others.

My mother-in-law, Regina Green. Thank you for your patience and understanding.

To my dear sister, Zeola Gaye. Thank you for your love and sharing your stories of my other siblings and father. Learning things about them has in ways helped me to understand myself. May God continue to bless and keep you, dear beautiful one.

With gratitude, Celina Inman, for embracing and supporting me over the years. We appreciate you.

To my cousin Takeia, thank you for being a loving, wise, and listening heart. Your love and encouragement have been a blessing throughout my life.

To all my family in Kentucky. I love you all. Thank you for embracing me and helping me learn the roots of Father's family.

To my dear niece Nona Gaye. Thank you for embracing me as your uncle, both privately and publicly. I am grateful for the laughter, tears, support, opportunity, and encouragement you have given me. WE have work to do.

To the late Janis Gaye, I thank the Lord for allowing me to meet and know you for a season of time. God used you to initially open the door to meet my beautiful family, those I knew of and those I didn't. You are/were family...my sister...we miss you!

To my grandparents, Eugene and Florence Martin, who loved me and took me in during my early and difficult teenage years. I pray to be just as loving a grandparent as you were to me.

Melvin Carey, you will always be my dad, our human protector and provider by the Grace of God. I love, miss, and understand you now more than ever.

My dear brother, Melvin Carey Jr., words cannot express how much I love you. It's hard to type these words without crying. I love you forever.

To my Children:
Chante, my precious daughter, though you are a grown and beautiful woman, you are still my baby, my little Tay Tay. You are a gift from Heaven, and I am so proud of you.

Continue to put God first in all you do. Know that as God gives me breath, I will continue to strive to be a godly example for you by the grace of God.

Antwaun Jr., I dreamed of you and wanted you before I ever met your mother. You brought me so much joy from the first moment I held you. You hold a special place in my heart. Know that you, my son, are loved tremendously by your mom and me, and by God.

To my Grandchildren:
Chloe, Antonio, and Christian. Grandpa loves you dearly. Know that Jesus is Lord and He loves you. Know that you have great purpose and were created for HIS glory, and you are to let Him shine HIS light through you. You are a gift from God.

With Gratitude: The late John and Lena Wilson and sons, Gloria Raines (my adopted grandmother) and the Raines family, Marla Peterson & Family, Tracey Cooke and family, Robin Terry, Rochelle Riley, Brian Stevens, Paul Barker and the family at the Motown Museum, Mayors Muriel Bowser and Mike Duggan, Synthia Fairley, Chelsea Smith, Minister Darlene Hayes, Patricia Canady, Paul and Ivy Bishop St. Ange, Dr. Lisa King, Renee Jemison, Yvonne Stewart, Jay DeJarnet and Family, Sgt. Jeff Newton, Captain Steven Carey, Steve Rodriguez, Celia Whitney, Charles and Treva Pettis, Shawnn Monteiro, Ronald Dearing and the Dearing Family, Saleem Hylton, DJ Gamel, The Late Gayle James and The Marquees, Lloyd Winston, Mark Gay, Bonnie Gay, Juanita Shanks, Nurse Taneyia Mitchell, Kristen Flath, Darrick and Quintella Butler, Robin Stoker, Robert and Kia Griffin, Dianne Allard, Patty White, Valerie Guyton, Rosy Rose, Lyndia Grant, Joe and Barbara Guy, Susan Smith, Cassandra Mason Outlaw, Beverly Lindsay-Johnson and the Marvin Gaye Recreation Center Staff.

Introduction

As I sat alone in the kitchen and watched the heavy snow come down, I began to reflect on my life as I tried to drown out the haunting thoughts that I was possibly dying. Eating a small portion of oatmeal had now become a struggle, accompanied by the constant discomfort of nausea.

Tears flowed from my eyes as I contemplated the possibility of leaving this earth prematurely.

Not because it was my time, but because of my sinful choices: not having fulfilled what I believed I was called or purposed to do. There were still so many things I had yet to express to my children about my childhood. To share my joys and pains, my hopes and fears, the supernatural things I experienced and witnessed, along with the last 10 years of struggles in my life, which negatively impacted our family.

I had not yet met my two living siblings from my father, Marvin Gay Sr., and I had so many questions to ask about them, our brother Frankie, and of course, the beloved Marvin.

I had yet to share the knowledge or insights I had learned that were supposed to bring healing and deliverance to many who were hurting, starting with my own family.

As I sat, battling the pressing emotions of despair, a song came on the radio with words that brought additional tears, yet also brought hope that directed my focus back on the lover of my soul - JESUS. The lyrics,

"And, though my heart is torn... I'll praise you in this storm,"[i] strengthened me. So, it was in that moment and in that lonely kitchen that this book was conceived.

This book covers 40 years of success, achievement, and victory, yet it also involves failure, loss, and painful trauma. Many of these moments were brought on by external forces while others were self-inflicted, hurting myself and others.

I did not create this book from a desire to be rich or famous, but to impart knowledge and warn and encourage family, friends, the Body of Christ, and the world.

Since writing the book, so much has happened in the last 14 years. Yet for now, by God's grace and mercy, I pray this book and my voice will be used for God's glory to help a hurting world.

"Determine that your future won't look like your past."
- Antwaun Gay

CHAPTER 1

FATHER... WHY?—UNSPEAKABLE PAIN

On Monday morning, April 2, 1984, my stepdad gave me permission to stay home from school. The exception was not because of sickness or problems at school. It was because events from that morning filled my fourteen-year-old self with unspeakable pain and confusion, and I needed time to figure out why my life had suddenly turned upside down.

Emotions I had never experienced before flooded my soul. Along with the rest of the world, I snatched a chair for support and tried to make sense of the news. Listeners from 96.3 WHUR kept calling the radio station to gather the latest details about the shooting the day before. Every caller was audibly upset with a mixture of anger and grief, while many asking the same questions over and over. 'Why would a father kill his own son? Why Marvin Gaye? Why this singer, songwritter, and musical icon? Why...?'

Radio stations across America planned on wishing the Motown genius a happy forty-fifth birthday that morning. Instead, the news of Marvin Gaye's death the day before stunned the world. The millions who were romanced, empowered, and delighted by his soulful voice froze with the realization that one of the nation's most beloved musical masterminds was gone.

The world clung to all they had left of Marvin Gaye—his music. Nearly every American radio station and household played his records and sang along in collective grief, all still glued to the news. Marvin's music changed their lives, and they demanded details about the man responsible for taking him so soon. As the news spread about Marvin's shooter, no one knew about the anger rising inside the singer's fourteen-year-old little brother. Marvin was shot and killed at the hands of a preacher—his father—the same preacher who happened to be my father.

I remember sitting outside on a kitchen chair, trying to process everything. I couldn't shake the deep sadness as I listened to the testimonies of people sharing how much Marvin meant to them, and the fury they felt toward Father. The perplexing and intense drama was too much for a young boy to handle alone. Yet there I was — sitting outside alone.

This was not the first time I felt alone. Loneliness began many days before while Mother was in the hospital. Now, the confusion and feelings of abandonment were magnified by the events of the day. She hardly spoke or looked at me during our recent visit to the hospital. I called to her,

"Mother! Hey, Mama, it's me, Antwaun," but there was no answer. When she finally turned her eyes toward me with a blank look on her face.

I was too young to understand what was happening to her. I just wanted Mother to at least smile at me. I needed her now more than ever to help me understand what was happening as I watched the whole world weep over the unnecessary death of my brother, all while rage increased toward Father, a man I had met just a few months earlier.

The news of my brother's death made me question everything about myself. My heart kept asking, "Why! Why would Father do that? Is he ok? Should I try to contact him? Is he thinking of me? Does he want me anymore? Would the family in California I heard about even want me? Or would my very presence serve as a painful reminder of Father's adultery against their mother? Would I ever see Father again, or would my first reunion with him be my last?"

So many questions swirled in my head, and I had no one to go to. I was alone again. The weight of these questions was too much for me to handle.

Doubt loomed larger than hope. I wondered if my birth family would ever accept me. I doubted the possibility that I would ever see Father again, that he would ever hold me or cry tears of joy over me as he had done the night I met him. As I sat alone that day, for the first time, I wondered who I was and why I was born. My brother was dead, Mother was in the hospital, and Father was in jail. I had no one to talk to. I had no one to share the pain, no one to help process my loss. I was lost. Not even my stepfather was there for me.

"Doubt loomed larger than hope."

Even though my stepdad had been my father figure since I was a baby, I didn't feel loved by him. He was a quiet, hardworking man. He put in long hours doing drywall work, so he was noticeably tired by the time he got home at night. Many nights, Mother waited for him at the door to greet him with a kiss of honor and to show her appreciation. But interaction with me and my brother, Mel, was brief. We greeted him with, "Good evening, Dad," to which he would reply, "Good evening." That was mostly the extent of our conversations and our relationship, except for when we worked with him on weekends to earn money, when we went fishing as a family, or when we all watched TV.

Any respect I had for him was built on fear more than affection. Harsh and sometimes violent arguments between him and Mother planted seeds of fear that would stay with me into adulthood. It was many years before I learned to appreciate him. In my early twenties, by the help of God, I could finally look past the hurt and neglect in my childhood.

Even though we had difficult moments, home was usually a safe place where we were provided for. But when Marvin was killed, I longed for the close relationship of a father more than ever. I was a teenage boy in need of a loving man to help me navigate the tragic news, conflicting feelings, and intense pain inside me.

Mother was also emotionally unavailable because of her mental health status. Before being admitted to the hospital, Mother was unstable and paranoid. She believed someone was trying to kill her, and that my stepdad was behind it. I was young and did not understand their history, so I wondered if maybe Mother was right. But, when she pointed to my brother and me as potential accomplices, I knew something was wrong.

Mother questioned me when I looked out of the blinds saying, "Who are you looking at?" as though I was in on some plan contrived to hurt her. One day in the car, Mother asked if my brother and I had someone following her. "What is happening to Mother," I wondered. "Why does she think I would hurt her?" A short time later, Mother was admitted into a hospital in Richmond, and I could no longer hear her beautiful voice singing Mahalia Jackson songs in the kitchen.

Even before Mother's illness, I sensed everyone in my home was perfectly aligned to each other except me. I was the misfit. Everyone's last name was Carey and mine was Martin, Mother's maiden name. When I was about eight years old, Mother told the story that changed the trajectory of my life.

Mother explained that my stepdad was not my real father, and that Marvin Gaye was my brother, but I was too young to fully comprehend what that meant. My first experience with Marvin was seeing his picture on an album cover I found in our basement at about that same age. He wore a distant, melancholy expression and a long black trench coat, just like Dracula. He stood in a somber background with snowflakes resting on his head.

I quickly put the album away for fear my stepdad would find me rummaging through his records. I wondered who this famous singer was. I had no idea how famous and beloved my brother was, or how I was related to him.

One day, I found a magazine cover with a picture of Marvin Jr. with his wife, child, and mother and father—my father—standing with him. I kept the magazine and took it out occasionally to study the older man wearing a vest and sunglasses. Father had no resemblance to me, but I dreamed of the day I might meet him.

When I lived in Olde Forge as a teen, I was teased badly. I thought I would win friends with the news that I was Marvin Gaye's little brother. I expected the boys to reply with respect and awe, "Really! Have you ever met him? Man, that's cool!" But sharing my family history only led to humiliation and pain when the boys bullied me even more than usual.

"You know d____ well that Marvin Gaye ain't your brother. Marvin Gaye? Marvin Gaye, the singer? Man, you're a lyin' somebody!"

"If Marvin Gaye is your brother, then why are you here in Virginia and why is your last name Martin and not Gaye?"

"Man, how old was your father when he got with your mother? She must have been super young."

I was too young to understand the complexities of my own story, especially the age difference between Father and Mother, so I shut down in silence and total humiliation. The confusion continued until Mother decided (with the help of one of her sisters) that it was time to meet Father face to face.

Nearly six years after I learned Marvin Gaye Sr. was my father, my aunt decided it was time I met him. She said Marvin Sr. was in Washington, D.C. and that he wanted to see me. A good, yet funny feeling came over me when she said I was really going to meet the stranger I called Father.

That evening my aunt drove me to Father's house in Washington, D.C. When she walked me to the door, a tall, dark-skinned man with a peculiar voice appeared—Father! I recognized him from the magazine! The wait was over! Here I was, 14 years old, meeting Father for the first time.

Father took me in his arms and held me tight, as though he never wanted to let go. He looked at me with tears running down his face. I sensed he had longed to see me more than I could have ever imagined. Right then, I knew that this was Father. I had never experienced a man holding me so tight and crying over me. "Father loves me! He really loves me!" He held me and looked at me as if he found his lost treasure.

He led me to the basement of the house and showed me around. I remember the ceiling being much lower than what I was used to in the townhome where I grew up. I was in awe of the house, but even more stunned by the way Father spoke to me like I mattered. He told me to make a practice of patting the skin underneath of my neck as some sort of beauty secret to prevent wrinkles. I thought it was strange, but I was going to try it because Father said so.

Before I left, Father showed me a watch and a ring he said he would give to me one day. He then gave me a one-hundred-dollar bill for my birthday, (even though my birthday had already come and gone). It was the first time that I had ever seen a one-hundred-dollar bill. Seeing and possessing it as a gift from Father was an experience I would never forget. I left him feeling so special and loved. I felt validated! There was no more wondering and doubting if I really was the brother of Marvin Gaye—it was so! Though I still didn't have all the answers, most of my doubts and the humiliation were gone.

Yet, there I sat on April 2, 1984, my brother's birthday and one day after his death, experiencing more hurt, pain, and doubt than I could handle. "Maybe one day," I told myself, "When I am older and famous for playing basketball, singing, or dancing, I will find Father and my family, and they will love me. One day I will go to Cali and live with them and become a star, like my brother. I will feel the same love the family had for him. Until then, I will have to make my way without them, until they call for me, or I go to them."

CHAPTER 2

MISFIT

Though I didn't realize it, I had already built sturdy walls to shield myself from loss and rejection even before Marvin's death. By the time I reached middle school, I had a long-standing reputation as a silly, hyperactive, attention-seeking kid. I was a black male in a predominantly white community. Just by my color and height, I stood out, and my impulsive behavior didn't help either.

The only time that I felt accepted by my peers was when I entertained them through comical imitations, singing, dancing, or athletics. The high of their approval fueled my passion to excel by being on stage all the time. I was afraid of either getting hurt or hurting others if I defended myself, so performing and making people laugh was a defense mechanism that kept the bullies at bay.

Scars of elementary and early middle school left me rejected and angry. I endured racial abuse from some of the white neighborhood kids who mistreated me for their own amusement.

In Stafford, Virginia in the 1980s, slurs such as 'jigga boo', 'porch monkey', and 'nigger' were common. Other scarring memories of cruelty from my peers include kicks to the pants, being forced to kiss a tree, and threats about the Klu Klux Klan.

Yet, the bullies were the same kids who wanted me to play football and basketball with them. Ironically, they celebrated my athletic abilities when our team won and blamed me if we lost. If I didn't play well and the team lost, I could be accused of throwing the game and the abuse rose again. I quickly learned that excelling in neighborhood sports was a must. The desire for friendship and acceptance overcame the hurt and humiliation. Looking back, I believe some boys genuinely liked me, but they were influenced and pressured by racial prejudices.

Another talent emerged to bring acceptance from both male and female peers. Motown's 25th Anniversary celebration was taped live at Pasadena Civic Auditorium in Pasadena, California, and aired on television on May 16, 1983. I watched Michael Jackson perform a few old Jackson Five songs before his brothers left him on stage to sing the best-selling single of his entire career, "Billy Jean."

Michael's black pants were hemmed short to reveal diamond sequined socks that matched his shirt, glittering like a disco ball against the dimly lit stage when he whipped out his right leg with a boomerang kick.

Then Michael Jackson changed both music and dance history in a sequence of just a few moves. He turned to the side, lifted his pant legs just slightly, and took us all to the stars with the silky-smooth Moonwalk, a performance that left the entire world either slack-jawed or screaming.

Michael Jackson's Motown 25th Anniversary performance lit an obsession in me. I spent the next two years practicing his moves, including his trademark sling-shot kick and his mesmerizing Moonwalk.

Along with basketball, I poured my heart and soul into dancing. I was obsessed with the way it fueled my soul, especially around the time of Marvin's death. My rewards were the attention, praise, acceptance, and self-worth I so desperately wanted.

I loved to sing, but I felt more confident with my dancing skills. I was rather good, at least in my mind, so I agreed to dance in front of the entire Gayle Middle School student body and staff. I had a small part in the music program, but my presentation generated a huge response. Every single one of the compliments about my dance moves stroked my self-esteem. Surprised students who mistreated or looked down on me told me how much they loved watching me dance.

I could change a person's countenance from indifference to admiration just by doing Michael Jackson's Moonwalk or his high front kick. Once I gained this insight, I embraced it with fervent zeal.

The silly black kid who had few friends and no girlfriends found a talent to bring accolades and win acceptance from my peers, regardless of their race or gender. My obsession with dancing became my way of fitting in and gaining the much-needed approval of others.

Both my peers and adults recognized my athletic skills as the key to my future success. I was determined to be a star, so all my time, energy, and attention were aimed at cultivating these creative talents. My bedroom became my singing and dance studio, as well as my athletic fantasy room. It was a place packed with an imaginary crowd for whom I practiced singing and dancing, running and catching footballs, or dunking basketballs. The world didn't know it, but Marvin Gaye's forgotten little brother was fine-tuning his craft and would one day emerge to be embraced and loved worldwide, just as his brother before him.

With my newfound success, I had a new goal. I dreamed of sharing a big house in Cali with my brother, Mel, just like Willis and Arnold on the TV sitcom Different Strokes. I knew this was my preparation time for the glory yet to come. However, I didn't realize my preparation would be met with obstacles and family issues more difficult than I could handle or comprehend. The mounting pressure would soon push me back to a familiar place.

I didn't realize my preparation would be met with obstacles and family issues more difficult than I could handle or comprehend. The mounting pressure would soon push me back to a familiar place.

CHAPTER 3

A DIFFERENT WORLD

Soon after Marvin's shooting, my attitude at school and at home deteriorated. As the anger intensified every day, so did my behavior. Several things set off my unusual conduct. One was Mother's mental status and continued absence. I believed my stepfather was the main reason Mother was sick, so I avoided him. That, along with the longing for love, guidance, and acceptance, created the teen I was becoming.

Even though I had never been obstinate or disrespectful to school administrators, something undeniable was happening within me. One morning, the vice principal of the middle school called me to his office. He had a reputation as a mean man, so his office was the last place anyone wanted to visit. That day, I did everything I could to appear unfazed by him or the threat of suspension. The vice principal was unaware of my circumstances at home, so he presumed I was trying to cop an attitude or act cool. Noticeably irritated by my lack of respect for him and concern for the consequences of my behavior, he slid his chair abruptly in front of me and leaned approximately eight inches from my face.

Anger, along with the longing for love, guidance, and acceptance, created the teen I was becoming.

Through tight lips, he sternly said, "Do you want to bump heads with me, son?"

Without hesitation, I roughly replied, "I don't care." That rude response was unexpected for both him and me. That was not the Antwaun I knew, but I felt like something in me was trying to take over. I was changing into someone I didn't know. I was in dire need of guidance and counseling. Instead, I moved in with my grandparents.

Arrangements were soon made for my brother Mel and me to move to Northumberland County, to the small country town of Lottsburg, Virginia, to live with our grandparents on Mother's side. You could drive from one end of Lottsburg to the other in a minute, but this was a place of refuge for me for the next three years.

Even when Mother was released from the hospital, I spent just one semester at home before returning to Lottsburg with my grandparents. Although I was thrilled that Mother was back home, my desire to live in Stafford was gone. I grew up fast in Northumberland County. Mother and the place I used to call home in Stafford weren't the same anymore, and neither was I.

My experiences during those three years shaped me for life. In Stafford, I was treated as an outsider. That changed fast in Northumberland. I was the new kid from Stafford, and although skinny and silly, my peers accepted me, especially those of my own race.

The Stafford neighborhood and school were predominantly white, so that influence permeated my clothing style, hobbies, and choice of music. I coveted Alligator shirts, Ocean Pacific shorts, and Dock Sider shoes. There was even an AC/DC Dirty Deeds Done Dirt Cheap album in my small record collection. The culture that was once my norm disappeared when I left Stafford. I learned a new normal in Northumberland, one that fed both my soul and my ego.

In Northumberland, my neighborhood was all black, I was surrounded by family, and the school had a larger percentage of black students. Suddenly, my Alligator shirt and belt were traded for AJ Styles and the rap group UTFO, which caused me to fit in and feel more comfortable and connected in my new environment.

Also, my music tastes changed from Casey Kasem's Top 40 to KISS 96 FM, a Richmond R&B radio station that introduced me to Melvin Lindsey and The Quiet Storm. My new preferred choice of music included LL Kool J, Whodini, Gap Band, Sade, Prince, and Trouble Funk's "Don't Touch That Stereo". It was a new normal for me and I loved it.

During that time, two new influences changed who I was. One was the experience of having best friends, and the other was getting attention from the opposite sex. Both impacted me positively and negatively. Both became the instruments by which I would share most of my ideas, hopes, fears, and dreams. Both would change my life forever.

James and Darryl were my two new best friends. I met James at school, and I met his cousin Darryl at church. Our vastly different backgrounds made us an unlikely match, but we quickly became inseparable.

James grew up in a rough environment. He loved to share how much he fought on the streets of the Berry Farm housing project in Washington, D.C. He was tough, and it showed through his rugged personality, street smarts, and martial arts skills, all acquired in the D.C area. The first time I ever saw a Chinese butterfly sword used with proficient skill was by watching James.

I had never known someone so proficient and knowledgeable in fighting at fifteen. I was reluctant to get into any conflict, but not James. I admired his toughness and kung-fu-theater ability. He was everything that I wanted to be—bold, skillful, and confident—and now he was my new best friend.

Darryl, on the other hand, was mellow and humble. He grew up in Lottsburg, loved Madonna, and played the piano for the church. He was the oldest and usually the most sensible, especially when James and I got into silly arguments.

Yet, he also he had a country roughness about him. Darryl was the most spontaneous of all of us. His adventurous side was evident the day he ran half a mile through a cornfield carrying his ten-speed bike. This exciting and carefree friend was exactly what I needed. Darryl helped me feel just a little less alone in this great big world of craziness.

Together, we would grow to be more than friends; we became brothers. We named ourselves the "Lottsburg Boys," or the "3Ds": dangerous, devastating, and deadly. Darryl was dangerous, James was deadly, and I was devastating. We were inseparable; people rarely saw one of us without the other two. We all were the same height and weight, so we even shared each other's clothes.

We spent our days laughing, sparring, playing ball, listening to music, and dancing. Thankfully, drinking, smoking weed, and cigarettes never interested us because we were always on a natural high. We understood that being cool had nothing to do with getting lit. Being 'sick as a dog' or 'puking our guts out' was not appealing to us. We also never wanted to be mentally or emotionally impaired, just in case we needed to fight or run (preferably to run as far as I was concerned).

Our theme song was "Friends" by Whodini. The lyrics deeply moved us because it seemed to be written about us. Every time the song played in the club, we put our hands up and acknowledged each other to let onlookers know we were one. We were loners whose personalities, likes, and dislikes, didn't fit into any group or clique but our own. We saw and experienced what other so-called friends could do to each other, and we wanted no part of it. We had finally found each other. It was as if God orchestrated placing us in the same town to experience sincere love and acceptance that would carry us through a trying season in our lives.

I knew I could trust James and Darryl and that we were the best of brothers. None of us woke up most days to a father who would still be there when we turned in for the night. Each of us had parental issues and lived with at least one grandparent. As true friends, we could be real with each other. When I told them Marvin Gaye was my brother, they never accused me of lying. Instead of cynicism, James and Darryl responded with remarks of surprise and interest. When they believed me and embraced who I was, I felt loved and accepted. I knew my newfound brothers wouldn't make me uncomfortable by making a big deal about it. I never believed I was somehow better than other kids, and I knew I could trust them not to spread it to other youth like I was looking for popularity.

In contrast, unlike Stafford, some in this small town where Mother grew up perceived something happened between Mother and the Gaye family. Some of the townspeople thought Mother had Marvin Gaye Jr.'s son. I felt confused and alone the first time a few people tried to confirm the rumors.

"Where you from? Who's your people?" a townsperson asked one day.

"Florence Martin is my grandmother," I replied, assuming they knew her as a respected teacher at the county's only high school.

"Florence Martin? Yeah, I know Ms. Martin," she said. "I went to school with some of her children! Which one of her children is your parent?"

"Sandra is my mother," I replied, to which another neighbor responded in admiration of Mother's beauty and singing ability. But then I was ambushed by the inquiring mind who made a point to ask the question quickly, while others were still around, a question that did not make sense to me.

"So, aren't you Marvin Gaye's son?"

The question caught me totally off guard, leaving me with no time to process how she knew I was related to Marvin. My anxiety grew as I noticed the others looked just as shocked and bewildered as I was.

In an attitude of disbelief, someone blurted, "Marvin who? You mean Marvin Gaye, the singer?" as they glanced at the questioner and then back at me to see if there was any resemblance.

Speaking softly and timidly, like a small child who needed permission from his parents, I finally replied, "No ma'am, he's not my father, but my brother."

"Ooh, so yawl had the same father?" she concluded, which seemed to clear up the misinformation.

But then, the inquirer asked one more question, as if to seal the facts in her mind, and make no mistake about who Father was. The question stung and brought a feeling of shame.

"So, the man who shot Marvin was your father!?"

"Yes ma'am," I whispered, trying to conceal the emotions surfacing to my face. Just like on other occasions, I was unprepared for the ensuing confrontation of questions about why Father shot Marvin and if he was really a preacher.

When I moved, it did not occur to me that I'd be living in the same town where Mother grew up. It was hard to keep secrets in a town like Lottsburg, especially rumors of a popular girl's pregnancy with a celebrity family.

It was moments like these when I realized how much misinformation about me floated around. Many years later, I still had questions. "What was my story? How did Mother meet Father? Did she ever meet Marvin? How did my aunt know how to contact Father to arrange my first meeting with him?"

I pondered these questions for almost thirty years before I gathered the courage to ask without fear of causing conflict and strife within my family. But the time finally came when I learned how a pretty little country girl's life changed one summer in another city and became forever connected to the Gaye family.

CHAPTER 4

PRETTY LITTLE COUNTRY GIRL

Mother was the first daughter, the second of seven children born to Eugene and Florence Martin. People who knew her as a girl described her as sweet, nice, and beautiful. People also loved to tell me about how Mother and her sisters could sing.

The Lottsburg community knew the Martin sisters as a quintet that could harmonize the sweetest of gospel hymns. I loved hearing Mother and my aunts sing when I was a boy. The sweetest gifts were when they spoiled me with songs written just for me! Yeah, they spoiled me!

The summer after high school, Mother went to stay with her aunt in Washington D.C. to make some money before going off to St. Paul's College in Virginia. However, Mother's plans soon changed when my aunt could not house her. Mother found a room for rent and went to check it out. The teenage girl knocked on the door only to be greeted by a middle-aged man in Bermuda shorts. She decided to check back later when the lady of the house was home.

Little did Mother know she would carry that same man's child within the year, the man that would become my father.

Later that day, Mother received a phone call from the man's wife asking if she was still interested in the room. Mother declined the offer, but what the woman told her next took her by surprise.

"Do you know who I am?" the lady asked.

"No ma'am," replied Mother.

"I am the mother of Marvin Gaye, the singer."

In an instant and without hesitation, Mother exclaimed, "Oh my God! I'll take the room!"

What an opportunity! How many young ladies would turn down the chance live at the same residence as the most popular and adored singer of Motown and the world? Elated, Mother went back to look at the room and found that the house was beautiful. Before long, she was living there.

Mother enjoyed living with the Gay family with the anticipation of possibly meeting Marvin. One day, Mother bumped into Marvin for the first time in the hallway. He had just stepped out of the bathroom wearing a robe. He paused and stared at Mother for what seemed like five minutes. Not a word was spoken by either of them. It was awkward and strange, but exciting for Mother to be in the presence of Marvin Gaye—Mr. "Heard It Through the Grapevine," himself.

Later, she heard the piano and found Marvin playing skillful, melancholy melodies. Marvin invited her to sit beside him as he sang about a girl named Tammi. Mother noticed Marvin appeared sad as he repeated her name so solemnly. She assumed he was singing about Tammi Terrell, who had collapsed in Marvin's arms when they were performing on stage in Virginia. Mother could tell Tammi had touched Marvin deeply.

These were just a few of the many memories Mother made that summer. She not only boarded in the Gay house, but she also accompanied them to dinners and events as if she were one of the family. The first time Mother rode in a limousine or ate lobster was with Marvin's family. According to Mother, she and Marvin's sister both ordered lobster that night, and Mother had to watch his sister to figure out how to eat it.

Father met my aunts when they auditioned for him. He was so impressed, he talked about them being back-ups for Marvin. However, circumstances changed, and that idea never came to fruition. Mother also told me about the night she met Kim Weston and Flip Wilson. Mrs. Gay asked Mother to serve them when they came to see Marvin. Flip Wilson shook Mother's hand but never smiled. She laughed when telling the story and said that she did not take offense or think Flip Wilson was a bad man, but she could not forget how serious he was.

The only other moment Mother shared concerning her encounters with Marvin was the last time she saw him. One night after arriving home from work, Mother bumped into Marvin in the dining area where he was eating. Mother was quietly ecstatic with the opportunity to talk with Marvin alone. No cameras, no fans, no distractions, just the two of them.

Although the conversation was entertaining and memorable, the mood shifted in one uncomfortable moment. At one point Marvin showed her a briefcase full of money. Mother felt an uneasiness that Marvin quickly detected. Mother was taken aback by the sight of so much money because it reminded her of the bad money she saw on gangster shows. The aftermath of such a sudden and awkward moment caused the conversation to fizzle, and they went their separate ways. The next morning, Mother heard Marvin had gone back to Detroit.

Soon after, Marvin went to Detroit, and Mother went to college reflecting on the unforgettable summer with the beloved Marvin Gaye and family. Of course, her story, and mine, didn't end there.

When Mother shared memories of Father that summer, she mostly spoke of his thoughtfulness, kindness, and generosity. It was Father whom Mother wrote to and asked for money for a dress to represent the freshman homecoming court at St. Paul's College. At some point, Mother left St. Paul College to live with Father and Mrs. Gay.

Somehow, Mother discreetly hid the pain and hurt she experienced with Father. Instead, she shared memories about how Father asked her about her life. He shared knowledge and advice as if he were counseling her. She recalled times they read the Bible together, and she shared memories of dancing with him; one time to "Suspicious Minds" by Elvis Presley. Mother appreciated that Father was both knowledgeable in the Word and a smooth dancer.

Mrs. Gay knew the day was coming. She'd even implied her suspicions privately to Mother, but Mother had no idea what she was talking about. When Mother told Father that she was pregnant, he simply instructed her to deliver the news to his wife. "Go tell 'Mother' that you're pregnant and ask her to forgive you," he told her.

Mother never imagined this would happen, but now she had been asked to follow Father's instructions. I can only imagine the conflicting emotions both women experienced at that moment. Mrs. Gay simply replied, "I forgive you."

Months went by until the time came for God to usher me into the world. The Cannady and Martin families were excited with anticipation for the arrival of the first male grandchild of Eugene and Florence Martin. The delivery was so difficult that Mother nearly lost her life. Yet the Lord kept her and allowed her to live. She named her firstborn son Antwaun Khristian Martin. Mother gave me her maiden name to prevent public scrutiny, and to assure privacy for Father and Marvin.

Father and Mrs. Gay came to the hospital and presented Mother with flowers. It was then that Mrs. Gay assured Mother they would help her in providing for me, but on one condition. Out of concern for both her husband and her famous son, Mrs. Gay respectfully asked Mother not to go public about my birth. Mother left Father's name off my birth certificate because if anyone saw the document the disclosure would bring attention to Father and Marvin.

As Mother honored Mrs. Gay's request, Mrs. Gay and Father honored their promise. They provided Mother with an apartment for a while. Mrs. Gay even welcomed me in her home to babysit me. She never showed hatred or animosity toward me, but understood that I was an innocent child who had no control over the circumstances of my birth. Yes, God, even amid confusion, used a hurting, yet sweet soul to keep and watch over me. Only God could do something like that.

When it came time for Mother to move on with her life, Father left her with some final words and requests. One request was for Mother not to be too harsh when disciplining me. This request came from a man who had raised four children and repeatedly told my aunt that he wanted more sons. Maybe he hoped to right past wrongs or that I might grow up to be a preacher like him.

Before Mother left, Father played on the piano and sang two songs as though they were parting gifts to stay with her and encourage her in the years to come. One of the songs Mother had trouble remembering and the other she wasn't sure about the title. Yet, she clearly remembered the words he repeated with sincerity.

"God will take care of you. No matter what the test may be, God will take care of you. Lean, weary one, upon His breast, God will take care of you." [ii]

As a middle-aged man, I sat in the kitchen taking in Mother's story—my story—as if I were a little child at story time. I pondered about how faithful God had been to Mother through her life. Yes, God had truly watched over Mother and the people dear to her heart. Yes, He truly kept Mother— the pretty little country girl.

CHAPTER 5

LIFE LESSONS

For most youth growing up, visiting our grandparents is a treat. They love on us and spoil us in ways our parents cannot. The hugs and kisses they give us, along with the money or candy they slip into our pockets, leave lasting memories that impact us for life. Since my already-spoiled-self lived with my grandparents and had two best friends, I was incredibly happy. Being the only grandchild living there came with many benefits that likely made me more spoiled than I already was. The greatest benefit was being able to hang out with James and Darryl for many hours at a time. We would often walk the country roads while talking, laughing, and scheming on how to get a relative's car. When we succeeded in obtaining a ride, we would dress alike and then drive to either Tappahannock or Richmond to dance battle and talk to fly girls. Both went hand in hand.

We always looked for the perfect spot to show off the repertoire of moves we worked so hard to perfect. We were competitive and always in search of a venue where we could dance battle.

Whether at the skating rink, the movie theater, outdoor street dance events, or clubs we had no legal right to be in, we never failed to find dance crews that were ready to battle.

The night usually followed the pattern set by the movies Breakin' and Beat Street. Either an individual or a dance crew would start dancing to draw attention, and soon a circle formed around them, like an enclosed stage with the audience up close and personal. We joined the audience to watch the dancer in the middle and study the reaction from the crowd. The music and the moment created intoxicating effects. My stomach always fluttered with butterflies, similar to preparing for a school basketball game. The sight of pretty girls in the audience only intensified the excitement.

Usually, another dancer jumped in to dance battle. The dancers who failed to meet the challenge left the floor in embarrassment and disappointment, while shouts of approval from the crowd fueled the performers with the confidence to take their moves to the next level. We watched until just the right moment and then jumped in ready to show off our prize moves.

James often started solo, but sometimes we started as a team to dazzle the crowd with our synchronized moves. Darryl would step in sometimes, but he seemed happier in the background hyping us up with a "Yea, Twaun," or "Yea, Fletch." Watching Darryl uncharacteristically jump in and bust a move only added to our intensity. We had many dance battles that brought out moves we had not yet practiced, which blew our minds. Often we could take an opponent's moves and do it better using their own moves against them.

The ladies loved it, which opened doors for dance opportunities we didn't have to ask for. Girls asked us, "What's yawls' name? Are y'all brothers?" Many nights, the dance king's trophy was a slow dance in the dark and a phone number to take home.

Slow dancing only watered the seeds of lust in my heart and became the training ground for my sexual experiences in the future.

Slow dancing in the country was far different from the Brady Bunch version back at my middle school in Stafford. It was up close and very personal. Unfortunately, it only watered the seeds of lust in my heart and became the training ground for my sexual experiences in the future. Experiences such as sensuous dancing gave me insight I wish I had never gained.

Embracing the romantic and sensual songs playing during the Quiet Storm radio segment brought about a metamorphosis that changed me into some type of Don Juan—at least in my mind. For every song that touched my soul, my mind produced a movie where I was the debonair Casanova. I instantly fell in love with the story in Teena Marie's song, "Casanova Brown," because I dreamed of being the suave guy who "had more girls than Howard Hughes had money,"[iii] yet without breaking hearts like Casanova Brown.

The girl I dreamed of resembled the woman in a song from the S.O.S Band called "Just Be Good to Me." My mental profile of her was not of a woman who was weak or naive, but one who would love this man and understand him. For her, something about him could not be matched by any other man, no matter how famous or rich.

I wanted to be the man who was loved and desired with the same passion she expressed in the song. Of course, later in life, I learned the images I concocted about relationships with the opposite sex didn't match reality. Even though I had relationships that came close to what I wanted, I found out that most of them more closely resembled the words in the song "Masquerade," "...searching but not finding" and being "lost inside this lonely game we play."[iv]

During these mid-to-late-teen years, my relationships brought both exciting highs, and painful lows. I found through my personal experiences that not every girl wanted a relationship. Some just wanted sex. I also discovered that sometimes I became emotionally attached much sooner than the girl did. Go figure...

My first date was with an older girl. She was an eighteen-year-old high school senior, and I was a fifteen-year-old freshman. Our date didn't last long, but it led to heartbreak. Our first date would be our last, and the experience proved to be a relationship learning ground for me.

We went to a local beach with my boys and their dates, but everyone separated so that we all could be alone. My date and I stayed in the car where we had the luxury of the Quiet Storm coming through the radio to set the mood I hoped would lead us to going all the way. That didn't happen because my lack of experience led to a change of heart I didn't expect.

First, the protection I had wouldn't work correctly. I definitely didn't want to catch something or get her pregnant. Second, two television episodes of Good Times ran through my mind the whole time. In one episode, J.J., got a venereal disease, and in the other, he thought he was going to be a father. Another hinderance was the song "Let's Wait Awhile" echoing either through the radio in the car or the one in my heart. Last, but most importantly, I knew I was going against God's commands. Deep down, I knew this wasn't right.

Apparently, my date thought differently. Her face quickly revealed dissatisfaction, frustration, and embarrassment. Whether she felt rejection, shame, or irritation for wasting her time with an amateur, I didn't know. Whatever the reason, she wouldn't tell me even after my continued questioning. Even though I felt as though I had done the right thing, the fact remained that not only had I forfeited an opportunity, I also lost my girlfriend. In fact, it got even worse. The car battery died and left us stranded for several hours, so she got home late, none of which helped change her mind or ease the situation.

Although, in my spirit, I knew the loss of the encounter was appropriate and right, I felt losing the relationship wasn't. I was hurt and second-guessing myself. Maybe I should've gone all the way so we would still be together. But I quickly wondered, "Isn't this the type of guy that girls dream of? One who is sensitive, romantic, and willing to take things slow? If so, then why am I alone?" Rejection had found me all over again.

Rejection had found me all over again.

That first experience caused reluctance six months later when two girls at a public skating rink sat on my lap (one on each knee) and kissed me. One of the girls had a warm smile and alluring eyes. Though this was the attention I wanted and dreamed of, it still just didn't feel right. Don't get me wrong. I was excited and flattered. I was also in shock, embarrassed, and nervous. A few teenagers walked by with surprise on their face. Some guys showed approval because they wanted to be in my shoes. Others looked on with envy and contempt as if to say, "So you think you're the man?" I hated being teased, but I hated being thought of as a conceited show-off even more.

To get out of the public view and be alone with these young ladies, I asked a casual friend if I could use his car. I got the ok, but before I could leave the skating rink, another guy came up as though he knew me and boldly asked if he could have a shot and take one of the girls off my hands. I was caught off guard by the awkwardness of his question and his friendly disposition. I paused for a moment and then reluctantly said ok.

To this day, I still ask myself why I allowed him to take one of the girls. Unfortunately, a few years later I would find out that this was one of the most reckless decisions in my life, a choice I would regret forever.

CHAPTER 6

NORTHUMBERLAND YOUNG BALLER

During my three years in Lottsburg, I grew from 5'9" as an eighth grader to 6'2" as a sophomore. I was tall, and thin, but I had ample strength, agility, and stamina. Just as my body and social life grew, my athletic abilities blossomed as well. Prior to coming to Northumberland, I found success in middle school sports in Stafford in both basketball and track. I led the Gayle Panthers to a middle school championship. I also earned three first-place medals in a track championship. These achievements gave me confidence, so I knew I would quickly excel in the small county of Northumberland. The reality was I would excel, but not quickly.

People underestimated me, and I used that to my advantage.

People underestimated me, and I used that to my advantage. I could dunk a volleyball and was close to dunking a regular basketball, so I assumed I would make the eighth-grade basketball team as a starter. Surely, once the coaches saw my ability to jump, it would be a done deal.

Reality hit before the first practice began. Though this small area seemed isolated from the rest of the world, Northumberland was filled with talented, athletic youth. During my first days at school, I took advantage of my lunch break to check out the girls and any potential athletic competition. I noticed kids in the country seemed to grow physically different than they did in Stafford. Even as kids in middle school, the bodies of both girls and boys looked like adults.

During my lunch break, my eyes caught two guys I figured had failed several grades because they couldn't possibly be my age. One was 6'3" and the other was 6'2". One guy had to weigh at least two hundred pounds. I asked around and found out they were not only in the right grade, but one was younger than me.

As tryouts started, I already knew that I wasn't the tallest, but I also learned that I wasn't the smartest, fastest, or the most athletic. We had three guys over six feet tall and dunking, and one of them was the best all-around player on the team. He and I would have a friendly rivalry while I was determined to surpass in him basketball IQ, skill, and athletic ability.

I made the junior varsity (JV) team as the sixth man. I hated that position because I didn't understand the value of my placement, but I didn't dare complain. I was thankful, but I knew in my heart that I should be a starter because of my versatility. I could fill in for every position except point guard, and I knew I could do that if they asked me. Nevertheless, I did my best with the role I had. I enjoyed being part of the first JV team in Northumberland County history to go 17-0. The victory was bittersweet, for although we had achieved our team goal, I felt that my own personal goals were stunted. Because of this, I resolved to work harder and make the varsity team as a freshman next year. It would not be easy, but I believed I could do it.

A year later, I arrived at varsity tryouts as a six-foot freshman with an improved game and higher jumps than the season before. My jumping ability matched a returning senior and the team's leading scorer. In tryouts, I handled my business to make sure my athleticism, conditioning, and toughness matched any returning upperclassmen. Although my playing ability impressed the head coach, it wasn't enough. He decided not to take a chance on playing me before juniors and seniors, or the starters from our JV team.

After the last evening of tryouts, the coach informed me I had indeed made the varsity team, but he didn't know how much playing time I would get. For me, that was just another way of saying that I probably wouldn't step foot on the court. During the previous season, I saw how little time he gave most of his players waiting on the bench. Although I was thrilled I made the team as a freshman, I loathed the thought of spending most of the season on the bench.

I spoke with my former JV coach, Mr. Bailey, even though he was not coaching anymore. He convinced me to look past the artificial hype of saying I made the varsity team as a freshman. I believed he was sincere, so I played on the JV team for the new coach. The cool thing was that JV games were played before the varsity games, so I took the opportunity to put on a show for the varsity coach and players. During the first two scrimmages, I led the team in scoring, and I threw down a dunk in both games. The basketball court became like a second dance floor. It was my place to shine. And just like the dance floor, I was cognizant of my surroundings, fully aware of the teachers, ballers, and girls entering or seated in the gym.

Where this awareness might cause most players to lose focus, I was never distracted. If anything, I was more focused. I did not want to disappoint or miss the opportunity to impress. I just knew this season was going to be awesome, and that all my hard work would finally pay off, but the season was short-lived. While my hard work was clear on the court, my lack of academic diligence was evident in the classroom. I spent classroom time playing around and passing notes to girls. This set me up for failure which made the season both the best and the worst of times for me.

I was kicked off the team after January exams. Hurt and embarrassed, I prayed and hoped I would hear of some type of loophole that would allow me to play, but no such news came. I was stuck. I could do nothing but suffer the consequences and strive to improve not only my game, but also my grades. I had to wait ten months for the opportunity to play again. Although frustrating, this was a necessary lesson that diligence in academics and sports both count.

Though it seemed like forever, the ten months passed, and I was more than ready to resume my journey to make a name for myself. By my sophomore year, I could dunk backward. I couldn't wait to show the coach and the other players. I made the varsity team again but as the seventh man. Again, I could tell the coach was impressed with my ability, but he was partial toward upperclassmen and returning players. Yet, he often kept me after practice while everyone else was dressing. He challenged me to do more jump shots off the glass and pushed me to explode off the ground. I suspected the coach was looking at future opportunities for me as a starter or even being the man, but that didn't resonate with me. I wanted him to give me the chance as a starter now!

Fortunately, it didn't take long before the coach was convinced that I was ready to be a starter. During one of the first few games, I put up some points and produced the first dunk of the season. I tried to play it off as though it was nothing but just a routine play, however, after hearing the first "Yeah, Twaun!" I couldn't hold back the little boy smile.

Keeping a serious and focused expression was almost impossible as I received praise from my team when I returned to the bench. It felt so good, and I wanted more. I wanted to do the same thing again, but this time against a better team—a team that had a more impressive crowd. I wanted to play our rivals, and that opportunity was right around the corner.

CHAPTER 7

THE RIVALRY

Soon after the season began, we played our rivals, the Lancaster Red Devils. Like most rivalries, there was a strong competitive dislike for them. That dislike could turn into fights after the game or on the weekends, especially if a player was dating someone from the opposite school, but it was the Northumberland vs. Lancaster game itself that made it a must-see event.

In my eyes, Lancaster had the best gym and crowd noise acoustics in the district. Whenever we played them, there was a big turnout from both sides. The bleachers were filled with relatives, friends, and peers. Fathers, uncles, and former players came ready to brag on their sons or nephews while confidently sharing their basketball knowledge, or the lack thereof.

Cheerleaders from both teams worked hard to pump up their school attendees. They also tried to outdo the opposing team's cheerleaders with unique and creative cheers. Fans for both teams boldly shouted their approval or disdain regarding coaching decisions or referee calls throughout the night. And as always, the school principal could be found standing at the gym entrance door talking to the deputy assigned to the game. The environment created an amazing place to show off my talents and win the accolades of many.

The atmosphere was so charged that I could barely control my breathing. Layup warm-ups was a time for a player to give a pregame show to the fans by showing off his aerial abilities. I wanted to both captivate the onlookers and intimidate the opposing team. My implied threat was for my opponent to think twice if he planned to meet me at the rim. My hearing and visual senses were so heightened, and I felt as if I were floating on air as my head came ever so close to the rim. The adrenaline was overwhelming. I just wanted this game to start.

Suddenly, the horn went off. It was time for both teams to go to their benches and prepare to battle. The show was about to begin. The starters stood around the half-court circle matching up to their opponents while the cheerleaders chanted, "Jump ball! Get it! Get it! Jump ball! Get it!" The referee blew his whistle, threw the ball up, and just like that—it was game on. Bring it!

Sometimes a man must be careful about what he asks for. Sadly, we were in serious trouble right after tip-off. We started off squeezed by a suffocating, full-court trap so effective that we could not get the ball across half-court. Every time Lancaster stole the ball, they scored, which only made the crowd grow louder. I never heard a gym that loud before. The pitch only made my heart beat faster. The volume left our entire team shell-shocked and confused. Coach soon called for a timeout, but he didn't quite know what to tell us, as though he was shell-shocked himself. He was loud, but he offered nothing useful for our predicament.

Even the best player on our team, whom I measured myself against, appeared to have the confidence sucked right out of him. I had never seen that look on his face before. He was a better player than he showed that night, but the coach didn't seem to know how to build him back up. Coach didn't realize the prized player he had in him, nor did he seem to know how to tell us how to beat the full-court trap.

His struggle became my opportunity to shine. Coach soon looked down at the bench and summoned me to go into the game. I kneeled by the scorers' table, hyped and intense, as I made a plan. Sometimes it's a blessing to observe before jumping into the fire of the game. When I got in, I immediately turned the tables by beating the trap and bringing the ball successfully across half-court several times. By the end of the game, I was the second leading scorer for our team.

We lost the game, but I was happy with my personal performance. My coach and teammates also took notice.

This was the opportunity I wanted, but not at the expense of my teammate. I wanted to outplay him, but not like that. I believed his poor performance was because of self-imposed pressure and the fear of being pulled out of the game. Despite his unsuccessful night, I had yet to beat him one-on-one. I was quickly learning that basketball was as much mental and emotional as it was skill and physical.

When the Christmas tournament arrived, one of our starters missed an important practice, so I got to start for the first time. I sensed my time had come, and I had no intention of giving the position back. The tournament was at our rival's gym in Lancaster and included two other teams. We were matched first against the Rappahannock Raiders. If we beat them, we would advance to play Lancaster in the championship game on the following night.

The stage was set. All I had to do was perform. However, the first scene included an interruption that would be a thorn in my side and a hindrance to my hoop dreams for years to come. While guarding an opposing player, I twisted quickly and heard an unusual pop. I thought nothing of it until I went up for a rebound. Moments later, my left leg gave away. I tried to shake it off, but I couldn't. Something was wrong. I couldn't run even though I wasn't in pain. I was out for the rest of the game. I went home dejected but determined to play the following night.

When I woke the next morning, my knee looked like someone pumped air and fluid into it. I thought it was just a sprain, and I would play regardless of the pain. Nothing was going to keep me from playing, or so I thought. No matter how I tried, I couldn't run or jump with the strength I needed to play.

The nickname "Devastating" fit exactly how I felt. I was distraught! Why? Why me and why now? I had worked so hard and waited so long! Why would God allow this to happen to me? Was it because of the new shoes? Was it because I was tired after chasing girls until three a.m. the night before? Other players were drinking beer, smoking weed, and doing other trifling things. Why not them? I did my dirt, but my dirt wasn't as dirty as theirs, so I reasoned with myself.

The following day, I went to an orthopedist and learned I had torn my anterior cruciate ligament (ACL). I was done for the season. I was crushed and at a loss for words. After orthopedic surgery, I prepared to return to the court. I thought the issues with my knee were over, but I found out years later that I needed so much more.

In spring, I joined the track team through the encouragement and harassment of a new coach. He challenged me in abrasive and unorthodox ways. Many times, I wanted to cuss him out and quit, but his unrelenting style helped strengthen my legs, and I went on to set a new school record in the 110-meter hurdles at the state tournament. The accomplishment helped ease my inner pain and foster a renewed hope for a promising basketball season to come. I would be faster, stronger, and even more focused on winning. I was ready and determined to unleash my frustration on any player or team I met.

Little did I know another life-changing interruption was on the horizon. In the new basketball season, God ushered a man into my life who believed in me and demanded more than any other coach before him. His influence gave me the maturity and confidence to leave my grandmother's house and to move back to Stafford. I was about to have an off season like no other, and it would be the most memorable summer I ever had.

Little did I know another life-changing interruption was on the horizon.

CHAPTER 8

THE COACH

During the previous basketball season, my school picked up a new coach from Suffolk, Virginia, named Michael Stevenson. He appeared cool, but he had a stern, tough demeanor about him. He had a noticeable, awkward walk because of previous surgeries. Before coming to Northumberland, he was the assistant coach for a team that left us embarrassed after the regional tournament.

I could tell he knew the game of basketball. He was like some sort of basketball Jedi Master. I learned he worked at the Five Star basketball camps, where he observed many of the best players and coaches in the country. After hearing about Coach Stevenson's experience and his descriptions of the great skill and athletic ability of players there, I knew going to the Five Star Camp was a must for me. It was the camp of camps. If given a chance to play there, I could get some coach's attention and make a name for myself. Coach Stevenson wasn't sure if he could get me into the Five Star camp because of timing and money. It just wasn't something my grandparents could afford. However, Coach got me into a camp in Frostburg, Maryland. I was so excited about going to my first camp that I didn't know what to do. I spent a lot of time thinking, preparing, and anticipating the experience. Grandma bought my first pair of Jordan's and I got ready to put them to the test.

Finally, the day came when Coach pulled up to the front yard and patiently waited for me to gather my stuff so that we could hit the road. Grandmother held me up with final instructions just as I was trying to get out the door. I responded with a facial expression and tone of voice that indicated I was irritated with her as I said "Goodbye," and walked away.

My grandmother didn't deserve my attitude. I didn't realize it, but I was spoiled, and my bad habit of talking back didn't go unnoticed by Coach. I opened the car door and placed my things inside and greeted Coach as I sat down.

"Hey Coach!" I stated, expecting to hear a warm mutual greeting. Instead, I was met with a firm and direct reply.

"Man, you kids today got no guts," he answered while looking at me in disgust. I just sat there bewildered, trying to figure out what I had done to provoke him. "You just had to talk back to your grandmother. Man, you got no guts!"

I was shut down before the car even moved. He would've smacked me upside my head if he thought my grandmother wouldn't have minded. Suddenly, I knew this was going to be a long trip.

During the drive, he explained how un-cool it was to treat my grandmother that way. This would be his approach throughout our relationship. He exposed my rebelliousness and spoiled ways in a point-blank manner and challenged me to do better. It was something I needed but didn't necessarily want.

Once we arrived and checked into camp, I quickly tried to get involved in a full-court game. The games currently in progress included campers from D.C., West Virginia, Maryland, Delaware, and other states. I saw the game as an opportunity to establish myself early and to evaluate the skills of the other players. However, there was one player who wasn't a camper.

Derrick was a camp counselor who played for Virginia Commonwealth University (VCU). His presence on the court instantly made me feel hyped. I looked for the first opportunity to guard him and to put his skills to the test. When the opportunity came, I successfully held my own against him. Even better, I think Derrick knew my skills matched his. For me, playing against him felt no different from guarding one of the better, older players back home, or the street ball legends at Brooks Park in Stafford.

When his turn came to guard me, I learned I could go past him and score a lot easier than I would have imagined. I realized that if I could do this to a Division 1 player as a rising high school junior, then two years from now, I could surely have a scholarship and be playing for a top university. This first game was a tremendous boost of confidence, which I used to help me against my camp peers during the week.

The counselors assigned us to various stations focused on a particular skill. I thought that I knew what hard work was, but that week proved me wrong, especially the defensive station. I considered myself good at holding the defensive stance, but that station pushed me to the limit. I always wanted to show my coaches that I had the most hustle and heart of anybody. Camp was no different. The consequence, however, was once coaches see what you can do, that effort is expected all the time. It is easy for a coach to detect when you are holding back, especially when you normally finish in the top three in drills.

The expectation of full engagement made camp extremely draining on me. Whether it was drills in the morning, afternoon, or evening, I had to give nothing less than one hundred percent effort. For me, that meant guarding the best player, scoring against the best defender, and out-hustling the best opposing rebounder. By day's end, I was too tired to enjoy the free time with the other players, so I either relaxed in my room or slept.

Midway during the week, I sprained my ankle. I was unfamiliar with sprained-ankle pain, so I planned on sitting out. When I told Coach how badly it hurt, he told me to suck it up. Whether or not he thought it was only a tweak, it seemed easy for him to say when he didn't have to play at the level of intensity I did.

I was about to sit out but changed my mind when Coach convinced me that my decision could determine whether I won the MVP award. That was not a chance I was willing to take. I returned to the court, gutted it out, and led my team to victory. When the end of the week arrived, I figured I had a good chance at winning the MVP and potentially the slam dunk contest. The only guy I thought could beat me was a 6'5" player from D.C. and in my mind, I had outplayed him.

The night before the championship and the dunk contest, Coach wanted to work with me on developing an array of dunks he believed would help me win. He was energized and ready to work. My mind was somewhat willing but my body, if it could have talked, would have exclaimed, "Are you crazy?" I tried to press through, but after ten minutes, I wanted to stop. Coach suggested some crazy stuff I believed was possible in the future, but not now. Once again, he questioned my heart and accused me of being a quitter. I was getting angry with this dude.

"Man, I'm tired! I can't do anymore!" I stated in frustration.

"Alright, quit then," he quickly responded.

I felt bad that I had let him down. For the first time, someone believed in me more than I did in myself.

For the first time someone believed in me more than I believed in myself.

I woke up the next morning with a renewal of adrenaline-fueled strength and excitement, as though I'd been given a B-12 shot. During the day, different teams battled hoping to win a spot in the championship game. After pressing through a few competitive games, my team made it to the finals and then took the championship. Soon after, I defeated my 6'5" opponent in the slam dunk contest, lifting off the ground as though I had extra air pumped inside my sneakers. A few moments later, I nearly cried for joy when I won the MVP award! I was the slam dunk champion and MVP winner at my first camp, and nobody could take that away from me.

Right after the contest, it was time to battle against the camp counselor from VCU. This was my chance to see what I could do against someone who played on a D-1 level where I wanted to be one day. I looked at him and thought, "He's going to have to earn this contest if he wants to beat me." But I quickly learned how an ego puffed up so quickly could be instantly deflated. The college challenger was given the first opportunity to start, and he wasted no time in showing me he was the man.

The first dunk he threw down made me want to sit down and take off my shoes in surrender. He smoothly, yet quickly accelerated from beyond the paint, pumped the ball between his legs, and punched down a backward two-handed dunk with his head parallel to the rim.

Reality spoke loud and hard in my heart, "You're still not as good as you think you are."

Coach knew this the whole time. That's why he pushed me so hard instead of taking it easy on me. He saw the untapped potential inside of me, but he knew from his experience that I didn't understand what it took to be great.

God gave me a coach and mentor who dreamed with me and was wise enough to check my faulty thinking. Coach pushed me to my limits to bring out the best in me. He did this all the while getting on my last nerve. I needed more than belief in the talent God blessed me with. God knew I also needed loving discipline.

When I returned from the camp, I was eager to show my boys and the coaches my trophies. My varsity coach, who I assumed would be impressed, seemed to care less. To my surprise, he displayed an attitude of indifference. He didn't know I wasn't the same kid who left a week ago. He didn't understand I needed him to celebrate with me. I'd received praise, accolades, and recognition from coaches and players from different states, but not getting his approval hurt. Rejection stung, especially from those closest to me. Even if it was unintentional, I felt hurt by those I thought believed in me.

Soon, a trip to a place I had once known as home brought a moment of affirmation that led to a new desire.

While visiting my parents, I heard about a camp in progress at Stafford Senior High School, so I went to check it out. When I walked in, I appreciated the beauty of the gym for the first time. It was better than the college gym at the camp. My old teammates from Gayle Middle School saw me and asked if I was coming back. I hadn't considered it, but they made me feel wanted. The coach of the team asked his players about me. Then, to my surprise, he let me play in a game against visiting players from Potomac High School. He matched me up against a 6'7" center even though I was only 6'2". I held my own and impressed all the coaches who were watching. The Stafford coach never tried to influence me to come to play for him, but he made it clear I should let him know if I moved back home.

I had to choose between staying in Northumberland or playing for Stafford High, a choice between two different places with two different receptions: single A versus triple A playing in a gym with one floor or in a gym with three. What should I do?

The last event of the summer was the deciding factor. Just before school started, I participated in the Hakeem Olajuwon (The Dream) A&N Slam Dunk Contest held at Forrest Park in Richmond, Virginia. Many college and high school participants were in the competition. One player was a 6'8" McDonald's All American from John Marshall High School and was headed for Georgetown University.

To my surprise and dismay, the VCU college counselor who crushed me in the dunk contest was also there. I thought if there were others like him or better participating, then I was going to be in trouble. At the same time, my renewed faith and confidence from my success in track and camp taught me that what seemed impossible could be made possible. I learned that "faith is the substance of things hoped for, the evidence of things not seen." Hebrews 11: 1 (KJV)   Faith was the key.

I came in third place, but I threw down my first reverse, 180 dunk to beat the 6'8" All American and propel me to the finals. Derrick, my camp counselor from VCU won the contest hands down. I now had another athlete to measure my leaping ability against. My goal was to jump like him before the upcoming season.

However, it would be a season where my jumping and other skills would be displayed outside of Northumberland County. I believed that to be more valued and appreciated, I needed to make a change. I thought playing in the Commonwealth District would better prepare me for my dream to play college and pro ball. Darryl was in the military, and although I hated leaving James and Coach Stevenson, especially before I could play in the Christmas Tournament against the Red Devils, it was time to start the next chapter in my life, a chapter I expected would be full of success and pleasure. However, I would soon discover that life is full of surprises and lessons still to be learned.

CHAPTER 9

THE RETURN

Moving back home to Stafford felt strange, yet pleasant. I left Stafford as a hurt, angry, and unpopular eighth-grade student, hoping to never return. Now, as a high school junior, I was excited about my future and eager to play where I first fell in love with basketball. It felt good being back with my family, especially my brother, Mel, who had returned to Stafford a few years prior. Mother still had her moments, but overall, she was in much better condition than when I left, and because I was older now, I could handle the mood swings better. I was thrilled she was home and smiling at me as if I were her pride and joy. It made coming home so much easier for me.

My brother was a freshman now, and though he seemed happy I was back, I sensed a certain maturity and independence about him. I think he was quite comfortable with the perks of being the only child. I loved him deeply and, though we weren't as close as I wished, there was a strong bond between us. Distance and time robbed me of knowing him better, yet I still held precious memories of picking him up and tucking him in bed when we were younger. I immediately thought of Mel and had to fight back tears every time I heard the song, "Just the Two of Us." Even as I write this now, the tears show up. Whew... I love that dude.

Anyway, I was not the same, so I anxiously anticipated how family and schoolmates would receive the new "'Twaun." Ironically, as far away as I thought I was from the past, it caught up with me in the most unusual places.

One day while getting a meal at a nearby restaurant, I ran into a familiar pretty face. Working behind the counter was none other than one of the girls who unashamedly sat on my lap at the skating rink. Her beautiful smile and irresistible eyes were even more captivating than I remembered.

We were excited to catch up, but she had to wait on other customers. We agreed to meet after she finished work. When we met up, we picked up immediately where we had left off, talking, and laughing as though no one was watching. We mentioned the crazy night at the skating rink, but we mostly discussed our present lives and how we both had changed. After a delightful evening, we decided to see each other again.

On our next date, she shared something that shook me in disbelief. Before coming to the skating rink the night I met her, her classmates accused her of sleeping around. She was hurt and frustrated, so she was tipsy by the time she arrived at the skating rink. She decided she might as well enjoy herself since her friends already believed the lies. At that moment, I realized the strong, overt flirting and advances that night came from a mixture of hurt and alcohol.

She told me the guy she left with that night raped her. She repeatedly told him "No," but he ignored her, and afterward, she chose not to say anything. My heart plummeted in disbelief and confusion. How could this have happened? I just didn't understand. I would never have let her go with him if I suspected he might hurt her.

My heart filled with fear and guilt. I could tell she sensed my anger rising as I mentally rehearsed the moment the guy asked me to take one of the girls off my hands. I was consumed with uncomfortable thoughts about how my casual decision set the stage even though it was his actions that victimized her.

Never could I have imagined this happening. Yet, the reality was that the ramifications of my decision didn't just involve a place, or a thing. My choice hurt a young lady I cared about, a lady who would become my girlfriend years later. I was afraid to tell her about his selfish request that night, so I just kept the ugly truth hidden inside.

Anger escalated within me as I thought about us and how bold this dude was to force himself on a woman and that he did it not far from me. What would I do or say if I saw him? I wasn't a violent man, but as my anger intensified, I wanted to release it through violence. Although he was older with the muscles of a grown man, I could not imagine approaching him without it becoming physical. I did not expect such an emotional drama when I returned to Stafford, but here it was.

The young lady and I dated for a short time. Although the relationship ended, the impact of that Saturday night would forever be in my memory. Years later, more women shared testimonies of sexual violence they endured from family members and other men they trusted.

I was too naive to realize how sick and dangerous this world really is, but through those private conversations, I realized violence against women is more common than I ever imagined. Maybe this was why some girls either became loose with their bodies or distant toward men.

I was too naive to realize how sick and dangerous this world really is.

The ladies' stories caused me to be ever more observant of potential predators around women and children. I had a new, heightened awareness when I saw a tipsy lady around other men. I was determined to ensure that every mother, daughter, sister, and niece would make it home safely. Always.

CHAPTER 10

NEW ADDITION

Summer ended, and my junior year began. Over a thousand students attended Stafford Senior High. My new surroundings were much different from what I was accustomed to, but the large crowd allowed me to slip into the new culture with less attention.

Old classmates were surprised and happy to see I was back. It was nice to see familiar faces, and I discovered a lot of my classmates had changed for the better. My time in the country helped me grow up, too. I learned life can affect and change us in ways we never expected. First, I no longer yearned for close friendship or for the approval of my peers. I already had those in James and Darryl. Second, I no longer wondered if girls would be interested in me. The attention from dancing and playing sports showed me what to expect. I also learned how a tinge of either vanity or insecurity can have a powerful influence.

Last, I wasn't giving in to the bullies anymore. I was still silly, and I didn't mind friendly teasing, but being bullied was not an option. I always hated violence, and I never wanted to hurt anyone, but I returned to Stafford with a new boldness. I was stronger, thanks to the influence of James and beat downs from some of the biggest and strongest country football players I had ever seen.

Before school started, I met a guy from my neighborhood named Cledith Lee. Everyone called him Lee. He was originally from Maryland, but he moved to Stafford to live with his aunt. We both had a friendly, silly personality. We loved singing, dancing, and basketball (even though he played in track shoes). My skills surpassed his in basketball and dancing, except we both imitated Michael Jackson well.

However, I had to yield to Lee's vocal range. He loved singing Michael Jackson's songs the most, but his imitations of Prince and Baby Face were very impressive. Lee also quoted many scenes of Batman from memory. I rolled around laughing every time he imitated Robin's catchphrase, "Gee willikers, Batman."

Lee was a good friend right from the start. He appreciated my abilities in basketball and dancing, and my approach with the ladies. Lee was like my biggest fan, yet all the while, I was his.

What I liked most about Lee was his appreciation of my faith. When he came to my house, he often found me listening and singing along to gospel songs by the Winans.

Gospel music was new to Lee, yet he understood I always wanted more of God in my life.

Though my lifestyle certainly had contradictions, I had a deep desire to know and to please Him.

Only James and Darryl knew how sensitive I was about God. Though my lifestyle certainly had contradictions, I had a deep desire to know and to please Him. Tears flooded my eyes every time I heard "I'm Lost Without You" by Bebe and Cece Winans or "Say Amen" by Howard Hewett.

The sound and lyrics of gospel music brought a freshness, conviction, and healing I just could not explain. It touched me deeper than any secular song could. Yet, when I listened to Marvin's music, I could sense his understanding about his own need for God. I heard it most when I listened to songs from the What's Going On album. Lee seemed to have that need as well.

We practiced both secular and gospel music almost every day, harmonizing our voices in the room and then performing them on the school bus to impress the girls. Deeper than the music, our connection was as if our souls were knit together, and the truth was he connected to my heart just as James and Darryl did. Surprisingly, I found another best friend.

CHAPTER 11

BITTERSWEET

Each day seemed to move in slow motion as I anticipated my first basketball game as a junior at Stafford High. The team had players with hustle and heart, but only few ate, slept, and breathed basketball like I did. We all practiced and scrimmaged hard to prepare for the clashes to come. I just couldn't wait to live the dream of being the go-to guy as the leader of a varsity basketball team.

Before I could lead, I had to learn new skills to adapt to the needs of the team. The coach made us practice a variety of good offensive plays, but I struggled. I was so accustomed to the freedom to maneuver from the offensive sets at Northumberland and playing at Brooks Park that the more complex offensive plays at Stafford were a challenge.

I had to learn to score with my back to the basket, which was not my normal scoring position. Our team lacked height, so to take advantage of my jumping ability, I had to work down low with the big bodies. There would be no more pushing the ball up the court and weaving through defenders. And no more defending guards full court and harassing them as they dribbled or shot the ball.

My confusion with the plays showed up as indecisiveness on the court, which frustrated both the coach and me. I was embarrassed because I wasn't getting it. Sometimes, I felt like I reinforced the stereotype of a dumb black jock—athletically gifted but intellectually slow. I knew nothing about different learning styles or types of intelligence—I just felt dumb.

Whether in class or on the court, these painful feelings cut into my self-esteem. I was self-conscious about asking questions everyone else seemed to know. As my embarrassment grew, so did my anger and hurt. I wanted to cry but I couldn't dare let them see tears—no, not even one. That would not be cool, and being cool was part of my game plan.

Before our first game, I envisioned a spectacular night. My mental scoreboard racked up 25-30 points, double-digit rebounds, and multiple blocked shots. I was ready, or so I thought. On the first play that I touched the ball, I posted up strong on the block. With my quickness and jumping ability, I grabbed the ball and went straight at my opponent with my almost-impossible-to-block signature jump hook. The unconcerned 6'9" defender knew this 6'2" center didn't have the vertical jump to clear his wingspan. He swatted my shot without even jumping. The guards consistently stripped the ball from behind as I tried to attack him. I scored only five points by the end of the game.

In a flash, I realized how an overconfident, trash-talking boxer feels waking up from a punch he never saw coming. Humbled and humiliated, I sat in the locker room in a daze and rode the bus home in disbelief.

In a flash, I realized how an overconfident, trash-talking boxer feels waking up from a punch he never saw coming.

I didn't realize it, but this game was one of the best things that could have happened to me as a player. The assistant coach warned me that if I didn't develop up and under moves in the post, then the big centers in the district would swat the ball to the wall. After games against teams like Osbourne Park, Woodbridge, Potomac, and Gar Field, the verdict was in. He was right. Yes, I was playing outside of my best playing position. Yes, I felt the plays were shackling me, but it didn't matter. Coach placed me where I was most needed for our team to win, so if the team was to be successful, then I had better start listening. I carried these lessons around with me for years.

CHAPTER 12

CLUB LIFE

Our team and my personal performance improved as the season went on, but it wasn't enough to keep us from plummeting to the bottom of the district rankings. We played hard, but we fell short almost every night because of our lack of size and basketball prowess.

Despite a losing season, I had a few victories. I made the Free Lance-Star All-Area Team, and I ranked as one of the top leading scorers in the district, even though I played with my back to the basket. I also had a few crowd-stopping dunk highlights. My favorite dunk was against the same 6'7" center from Potomac High School who I had guarded at camp, as I jumped so effortlessly from behind the dotted line.

Other than my personal success on the court, the only reprieve I had from the dismal season was in the club. The club life was my other pastime, and it was going much better than the basketball season. Interestingly, I got a lot more attention for my dance moves at the club than I did for my moves on the court.

Mel, Lee, James, and I attended a teen club called "Impressions," and it certainly lived up to its name. Impressions had a movie-club style more common in the Big Apple than in Stafford, Virginia. It had a sweet dance floor with a video screen to entertain the regulars who came from Washington and Northern Virginia. The big-city flair and sophistication of Impressions also made it a popular spot with pretty ladies from all over the region.

During my junior year, I found the most success on my second-favorite stage, the dance floor. James and I quickly made a name for ourselves as two of the best male dancers at Impressions. The amount of respect and jealous looks we got from other guys, as well as the phone numbers and dance opportunities we gathered from the "Tenderonies," allowed us to show off our moves all night long.

We saved our best routines for the dance battles in the cypher, where the "Oohs" and "Ahhs" of the crowd always determined the winners. Nothing was more satisfying to me than to see our opponents perplexed by moves for which they had no answer. As they watched us dance, their faces dropped in noticeable defeat. Our synchronized popping moves, with a twist of ballet, specialized martial arts, and current popular dances, were just too much for our competition. Some opponents just tapped us and said, "You got it this time," while the faces of others would heat up as they grit their teeth.

> Nothing was more satisfying to me than to see our opponents perplexed by moves for which they had no answer.

The DJ announcing my arrival and appreciative pats on the back from the crowd only fueled my desire to please even more.

This warm reception and recognition was a dream come true for me. I often wondered if Marvin was also driven to perform by the pleasure of recognition, but, of course, on a much larger scale. I envisioned him displaying a smooth, debonair manner, and enjoying his choice of women, while other men looked on in envy. My experience at the club was an addicting one, and it felt much better than the days when girls weren't attracted to me. If this was how Marvin felt, then I couldn't wait to get to his status. If only, I dreamed, he could see his little brother following in his footsteps.

As quickly as I imagined these scenes, I had to shut them down when the painful past resurfaced and sadness overcame me. Moments of wondering about Marvin, his life, and my connection to him sprang up in the car, in my room, and even in a crowded club. I also wondered if Father missed me and yearned to be reunited. Every time my thoughts wandered to Father, I had to come back to the present to dodge the onslaught of sweeping pain. I kept all those questions and feelings suppressed since the day of the shooting. It worked so far, and I didn't want to get overly sensitive now. There was already enough disappointment to endure, and though it would be about nine months later, more trouble was right around the corner.

CHAPTER 13

WHY ME?

A life of girls and clubbing kept me in constant motion, but I began to wonder about my life just as the basketball season ramped up again. I sat in the locker room minutes before the season's first game, meditating and focusing on what I thought was going to be a forty- or fifty-point night. I reflected on my successes: making the All-Star team, my improved performance, and another crowd-stunning dunk I made at Southern Stars camp in North Carolina.

I tried not to think about how I re-injured my knee at another summer basketball camp just a few months earlier. I also tried to forget about the lost opportunity to compete with the best in the country at the Five-Star Basketball Camp. Those losses were devastating, but I couldn't think about that now. Now was the time to focus on the game at hand and how I was about to unleash my anger on the other team.

Although my knee wasn't fully recovered, I thought I was physically more prepared than the year before, thanks to street ball battles where I was now dunking on grown men at Brooks Park. I spent the end of summer and the start of fall playing against older street ball legends, so I was confident no one could stop me. This was my senior year, and I was determined to set things off by sending a message to the entire league. The only thing I needed now was for the horn to blow, the referee to throw up the ball, and I could handle the rest.

The buzzer sounded, the crowd cheered, and everything was going as I had envisioned for the first ten minutes. I grabbed nine rebounds and scored eighteen points, including a slam dunk three-point play. Yea! It was on! What better start than this, fulfilling my goals and dreams, right in my home gym. Confidence flooded my soul as I played with all the effort I could.

Then the unthinkable happened. POP! AAARGH!!!

Screaming, I held my knee and rolled on the floor in excruciating pain! I felt it shift in a freaky manner as ligaments stretched. I wailed in agony while pounding the floor over and over as coaches and trainers tried to keep me calm. Their efforts to comfort me were to no avail as the pain I felt in my heart drowned out all consolation.

In my heart, I kept asking, "Why God? Why me? I don't drink, I don't smoke, or do drugs; I don't start fights, but I try to prevent them! I pray to You and I read my Bible at times. I just don't understand!"

It seemed as if God didn't care.

But all I heard was silence. No matter how many questions I asked Him, there was nothing but silence. It seemed as if God didn't care. I was hurt and confused about why God would allow this to happen, yet I didn't dare entertain the thought of being angry with Him, although deep down, I might have been. I reasoned it must be a test of my faith—a hard test—but just a test; however, the tests kept increasing in frequency and intensity.

I sat out only seven games before I foolishly got back on the court in time to put up a couple of thirty-point games. I did not realize that playing with a large metal knee brace was not smart and was putting any chance of having a college or pro career in jeopardy.

After the season ended, I hurt my knee again, but this time, it was so bad I couldn't walk. I had to choose between walking with a limp or surgery. The doctors said my prognosis to play college ball was good, so I chose surgery to finally repair my ACL. I rehabbed for about two months until I couldn't afford the treatment anymore and then tried to rehab by myself.

Only six months after my surgery, I made another unwise decision. I tried out for the Northern Virginia Community College basketball team. I made the team, but halfway through the season, I had to stop playing because of the constant swelling in my knee. The storms just wouldn't stop.

Within a year and a half, I had experienced the loss of my first love, the loss or delay of my college career, and after a crazy situation, my trust in my best friend James. This was the season in my life where I had expected to truly come into my own, but I was losing more than I was gaining. I expected to have a scholarship and to play at a major college. I thought I would be on TV with all the attention and fulfillment that come with being a college star.

This was supposed to be the time when my vocal and dance fame would reach far beyond Virginia all the way to my family in California. They would somehow hear about me, and it would bring a smile to Father's face. Instead, many nights, I soaked my pillow with tears. I felt so alone. Everything and everyone I put my hopes in let me down. I felt like some invisible force was laughing and delighting in my confusion while all my dreams slipped away. I was only nineteen, and I was already stuck in a crazy maze I couldn't get out of.

I felt like some invisible force was laughing and delighting in my confusion while all my dreams slipped away.

Standing outside of a club one night, I recalled a conversation with James about the many women admirers we had inside and how crazy it was. In a quick moment of reflection and introspection, I realized I wasn't as happy as I thought I would be.

The attention and approval I always yearned for wasn't fulfilling because the satisfaction was vain and fleeting. I realized that more women, more clubs, and more attention didn't help or stop the emptiness inside when a crisis came.

Those amusements could not dig deep enough to penetrate my loneliness, to heal my knee, or to restore my dreams.

In all the chaos, there was a significant, yet still, small voice saying, "Stop and come to Me." When times of fear and pain came, there were always two people I thought about most, God and Mother. Though these were not the only times God entered my thoughts. A crisis seemed to bring on thoughts of Him more and more, and I needed His help and peace now like the first night I met Him.

CHAPTER 14

JESUS SAVES

When I was about twelve, Mother took me to a revival one night at an Assembly of God Church in Stafford. The preacher and most of the congregation was white. Not that it mattered, but most people were black at other churches I'd attended. I learned from Mother that the color of the pastor and congregation didn't matter. What mattered was that the true Word of God was being preached. What mattered to Mother was her growth and that her family was saved by surrendering their lives to the Lord.

That night, the Word of God moved me in a way that pierced my heart. Yes, I heard impactful messages from preachers before, but this time it took a hold of me differently. The message the minister shared pricked my heart so I wanted only three things: I wanted to be forgiven of my sins, to not go to hell for all eternity, and to surrender my life to the One who loved me so much that He suffered and died on the cross to save my soul. I wanted to live for the One who was raised from the dead, the One who defeated death and the grave. I believed that Jesus was, and still is, Lord. I was nervous, but not enough to keep me from answering the preacher's invitation to come to the altar.

With my heart pumping, I answered the call and made the long, intimidating walk to the front of the church. I kneeled at the altar with tears streaming down my face. Although I was a preteen who wasn't shy about acting out in a classroom or performing on the sports field, drawing attention to myself in a church made me very uncomfortable. I avoided drawing attention in church like lashes from Mother's belt.

Still, that night, I was so overwhelmed with what Jesus did for me, that I wept uncontrollably. I believed the Word and I desperately wanted Jesus to save me. With hands stretched out and calling for Him, the most peculiar thing happened. I started speaking words that were not normal. I was so embarrassed when Mother spoke words like that, yet, this phenomenon I so despised happened to me that night. A language and tongue I never uttered before flowed eloquently from my lips!

I was so overcome in an inexplicable, personal, spiritual encounter with the presence of God that I was oblivious to the crowd. An abundance of peace overtook and comforted me. On the bus trip back to our car, all was at rest as I gently lay in Mother's arms. In gratitude for what He had done for me, I didn't want to move or talk. This was the most memorable and peaceful night of my life, and I just wanted the serene feeling to stay with me forever.

This connection with God was the deepest part of me, yet I tried to hide it through middle school and high school. His presence within me was both a positive hindrance and a protectant as I participated in my teenage playboy activities. His voice deep within me often prompted me to leave the middle of the dance floor. I remembered the Scripture that Jesus would come like a thief in the night, so I wanted to listen and embrace the Gospel instead of the secular. But even though this was the real me, it seemed too weak to overcome my sinful desires.

As my high school years continued, I found that I was progressively becoming more affected by the pride and lust of the world. My elevated pride made it harder to resist a challenge to a fight, and I was increasingly pulled down by lust. I sensed God warning me that I would die if I didn't change my lifestyle. At first, it was a small voice I tried to ignore, but now it seemed continued storms were shaking my life.

One storm was a bad car accident after I left a club. I prayed and asked God to take away all that was wrong with me and help me resist the things my flesh enjoyed but were displeasing to Him. Just to drown out all doubt, I asked Him to save me again. All I knew was my way wasn't working, and that I didn't want to die before my time. I realized that I desperately needed God's help to live in a way that was pleasing to him. I wanted to be a real Christian.

I had an increase awareness of my sin and my need for God during and after my knee surgery. I cried out to God several more times, and I constantly listened to the Winans. God used their music to strengthen, comfort, and convict me. More importantly, I prayed more and read the Word of God like never before. With the help of the Holy Spirit, God's Word impacted my thinking and changed my behavior.

The turnaround in my life affected my relationships, especially my relationship with a young lady I genuinely cared about. As I wanted more of God, I saw the connections between my obedience to Him and the fulfillment of my dreams.

She didn't realize just how much I was changing until I told her I wanted to chill from having sex. I knew that speaking those words was a miracle only made possible by the power of God. I felt a strength and newness that could only be compared to the special revival night when God first touched me.

I was changing for the better, but it came at a price. Our conflicting desires led to the day I had to choose between pleasing her or God. By God's grace and help, I chose Him. It wasn't easy but I chose Him at the cost of losing her.

On our last day together, we spent hours talking at her house. I hoped she would change her mind and join me on my journey, but that was all just wishful thinking. She made her decision, we got in her car for the last, difficult drive back to my grandmother's house. As she pulled out of the driveway, I stared out the passenger window to hide the tears rolling down my face.

I was changing for the better, but it came with a price.

A Winans song dropped into my heart, and the words permeated into my ears and saturated my heart, "If you love Me, why don't you give Me you? If you need Me why won't you give Me you? I'll give you everything... if you give Me you. You can do anything if you give Me you."[v]

I believe it was the Lord distinctly speaking to me through the lyrics of the song. I realized the present suffering couldn't be compared to the blessings God had for me, so I had to let go of anything or anyone that hindered my walk with Him. This decision changed my life and drew me closer to God.

A week later, I told James that unless he could take nails in his hands and feet and give me eternal life, I could no longer go to the club. He said nothing, his silence told me he couldn't fill those shoes. My days of clubbing were over.

As I quietly reflected about the newfound joy and strength that had come upon me, tears of suffering gave way to a little-boy-smile. I was changing and things would never be the same. Yes, brighter days were ahead, I just knew it.

CHAPTER 15

THE AWAKENING

I couldn't believe I was back at home with my parents in Stafford, but it was even more surprising when I was home most Friday and Saturday nights. It caught Mother off guard to see her son home instead of getting ready to go out. As with most Christian mothers whose sons are going the wrong way, Mother had been praying for me for years. She prayed I would stop hanging out on the streets and surrender fully to the Lord. I believe she called the 700 Club for me so many times that my name was probably on their all-time call-in prayer list. Now she was seeing the fruit of her perseverance. Her son was home instead of chasing girls and clubbing the night away.

Mother didn't know why I backed off on clubbing, but she gradually witnessed the change in me. She knew something was different when I stayed home on the weekends, instead of obsessing over getting my hair cut, and dressing to impress while my stereo set the mood for the night.

Now, Mother saw me sitting in the living room wearing casual clothes, watching TV, and occasionally going outside to sit on the step. Staying home wasn't easy at first. I would get so fidgety; I didn't know what to do with myself. Since the age of fifteen, there were very few weekends I stayed home, and even fewer weekends when I was alone.

Now, I paced the living room, watched the clock and looked out the window as though a car was going to pull up with one of the guys asking me if I was ready to go. When my watch showed ten p.m., it usually meant it was time to leave, but now I was just hanging out at home while those in the club could only reminisce about the slender, goggle-wearing, bow-legged dude who would dance all night.

The next significant change Mother witnessed was a new diet of Scripture and Christian ministry television to feed my soul. Like a newborn baby craves the taste of milk, my spirit craved for more of the Bible as I read it. I was blown away as I read the amazing stories and pertinent topics from the Bible. Other than going to church, the one thing necessary to truly give God all of me was to read the Bible.

Other than going to church, the one thing necessary to truly give God all of me was to read the Bible.

Mother set an example to teach my brother and me that the Bible is important. Sometimes she told us to read our Bible before we could play outside or watch TV. She spent a lot of time in the Word, filling her Bible with notes and underlining verses that were dear to her heart. To me, Mother was like a super-Christian. She was a giving woman who devoutly read her Bible, prayed, watched the 700 Club, and sang hymns around the house. Every Halloween, Mother kept the porch lights off to dissuade people from coming by. If anyone came to the door, she gave them Bible tracks. She was truly a believer and understood the Word of God well.

As I read the Bible, it didn't take long to see a lot of my questions about life were clearly answered inside its pages. I was also amazed at how the Bible spoke on issues I never heard preached but applied to my life and generation. Moses's anger, David's lust, Jeremiah's insecurity, a few prophets' wishes to die, and Peter's anger and hypocrisy regarding the Gentile believers all caught me off guard. The more I read, the more I became intrigued.

Illumination filled my mind while a strong conviction flooded my heart. On numerous occasions I was so overwhelmed by the living Word that I felt like I would explode. At other times I would cry with the realization that the God of all creation was revealing Himself to someone so undeserving as me. I knew without a doubt that the Bible was the living Word of God and any believer could understand and interpret Scripture properly with the help of the Holy Spirit.

I was finally awakening to the fact that I lived a lie through most of my life. I learned there was a real matrix with a real enemy, an enemy that wanted me to spend my life perpetuating and trafficking his lies. This adversary tried to get me to support him and his evil world system so I would leave this earth without knowing my true purpose.

I prayed God would give me a pastor after His own heart, a pastor who would teach me and feed me with knowledge and understanding. Shortly after my prayer, I found at least three pastors on TV that I sensed God was using to answer my prayer. One of those pastors preached a message to transform my thinking and expose even more distorted beliefs, especially the religious and racial lies I absorbed.

But God wasn't finished. One of those pastors preached a message to transform my thinking and expose even more distorted beliefs, especially the religious and racial lies I absorbed.

I saw clearly just how deceived I was, along with most other Christians of all races. While listening to the messages, I realized I was part of a generation of young, black males who were brainwashed by the media through both overt and subliminal messages to define who we are and what we should aspire to. I never thought about the fact that most of my black role models either played sports, sang, rapped, or danced. Sports media inferred a black man like me could be a football running back or receiver, but not a quarterback. The media told me I was athletically gifted, but intellectually slower than my white counterparts.

I was also enlightened to the fact that my society did very little to show, tell, or highlight the achievements or contributions of blacks throughout the history of the church, the United States, or the world. If African Americans were acknowledged for our contributions, it would correct the thinking of our youth and strengthen the self-esteem of my entire generation and generations to come.

It had never before occurred to me that when I heard the word angel, I automatically imagined a white angel. I never questioned why I didn't see an angel as any other color. I also realized why it was forbidden to teach a slave how to read and write. Knowledge is powerful, but especially understanding from the Word of God, because truth exposes lies, whether cultural, historical, educational, racial, political, or religious.

For most of my life, I used all my energy and strength to excel with my athletic and artistic talents, but I neglected my spirit and my mind. I was misguided, misinformed, and motivated to focus on the wrong things. Yes, I was conditioned and programmed to love and worship human-glorified creatures over the Creator.

How much time had I wasted? How many young men like me were running after money and fame, going to prison, or dying in the streets. How many other youths were depressed and confused, thinking that power, position, money, or suicide were the answers to their pain? How many singers began in the church only to yield their voices to this world's secular system that provided no eternal value?

How many other youths were depressed and confused, thinking that power, position, money, or suicide were the answers to their pain?

My self-worth couldn't be found in clothes, money, fame, or in another man's opinion. God already declared I was valuable, and His wisdom and understanding would make up for any intellectual deficiency I might have. Yes, "God hath chosen the foolish things of this world to confound the wise." 1 Corinthians 1:27a (KJV)

Tears once again flooded my eyes as I thought about how blessed I was to have escaped the madness, and yet I remembered the millions still trapped. I grew furious at the thought of how the devil tried to destroy me, and how he attacked Mother with stress and fear over the years. He robbed me of ever getting to know my brothers Marvin and Frankie and of spending time with Father. Without knowing all the details of their life struggles, I now knew the master orchestrator behind my family's drama and tension. It was the evil one himself.

I never imagined I'd have this kind of awareness by the age of twenty. My dreams of playing ball in the NBA were still very much alive, but I saw that aspiration through enlightened eyes. If I was to play in the NBA, it would be to God's glory and not mine, and for the uplifting of others rather than myself. Young and still in a new relationship with the Lord, I eagerly longed to witness to others by sharing what I learned about God. I felt the burden to sound the alarm and expose the lies, so much so that I would soon find out that even without a license or a seminary degree, God was preparing me for the mission field in the most needful of places.

My Father, Marvin Gay, Sr.

Antwuan and Antwaun , Jr.

Heading out!

"What Are We Going to Do?"
-Initial Sermon

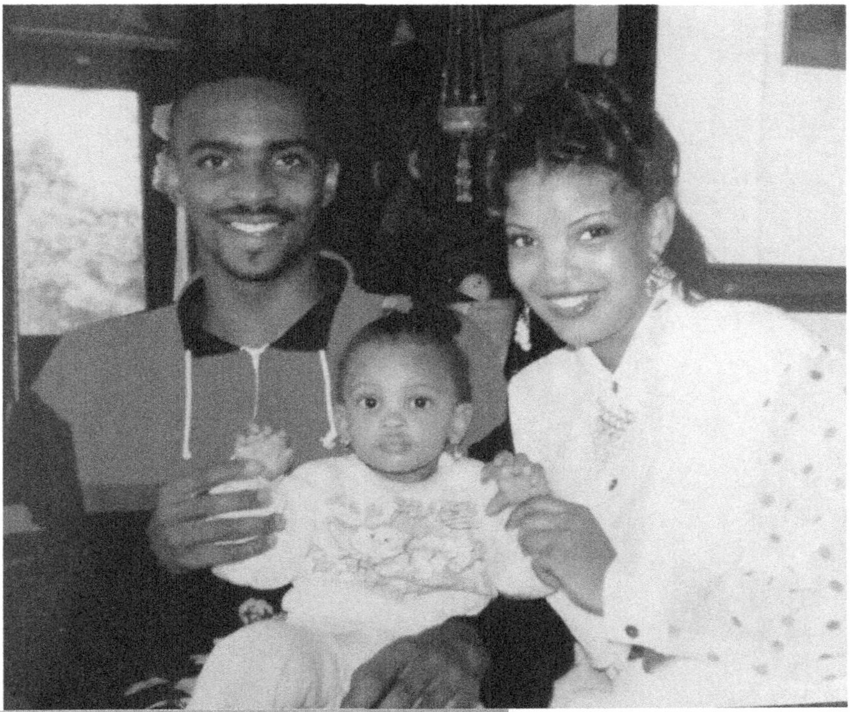

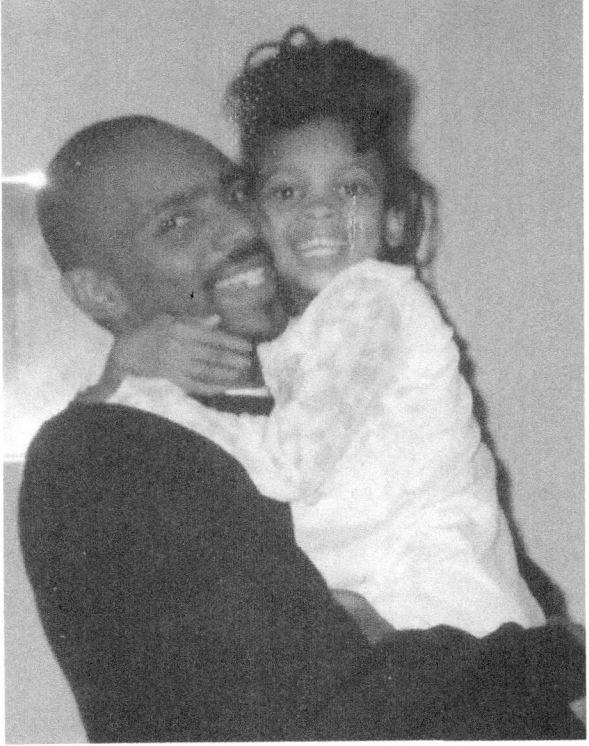

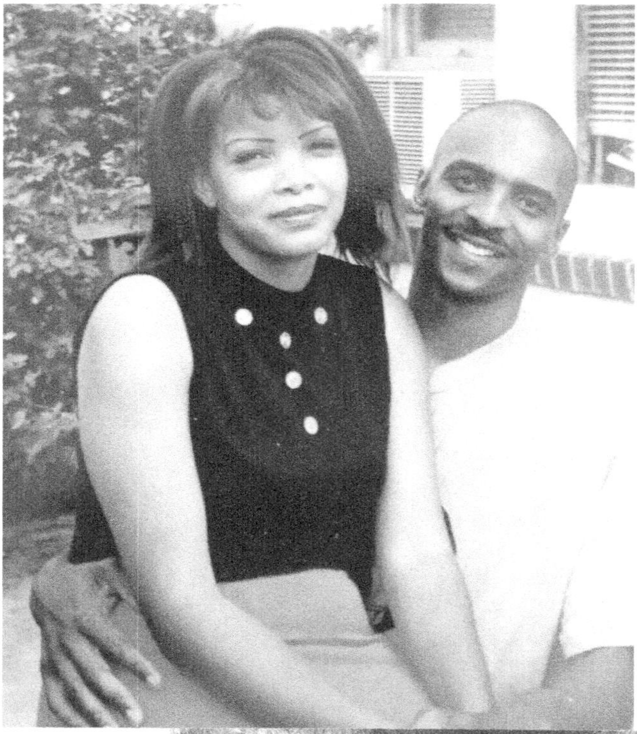
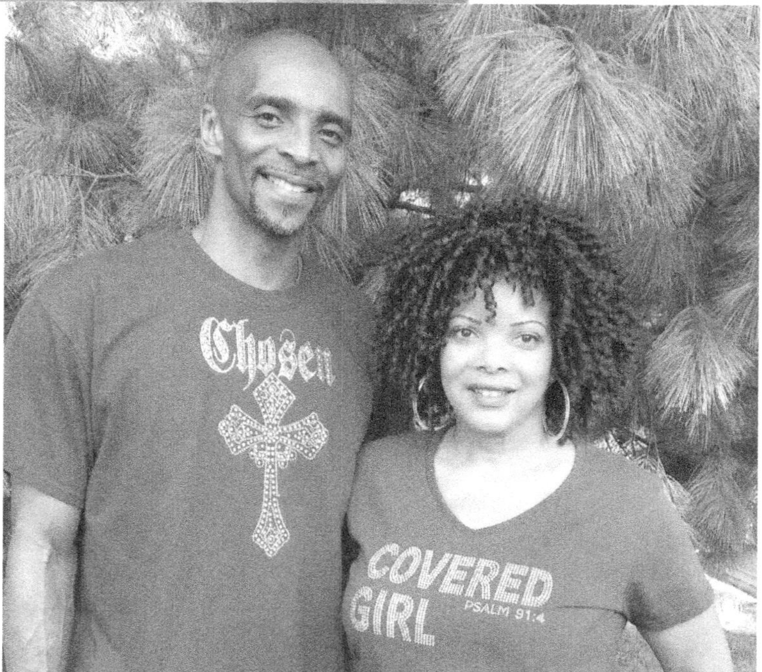
Chosen
COVERED GIRL
PSALM 91:4

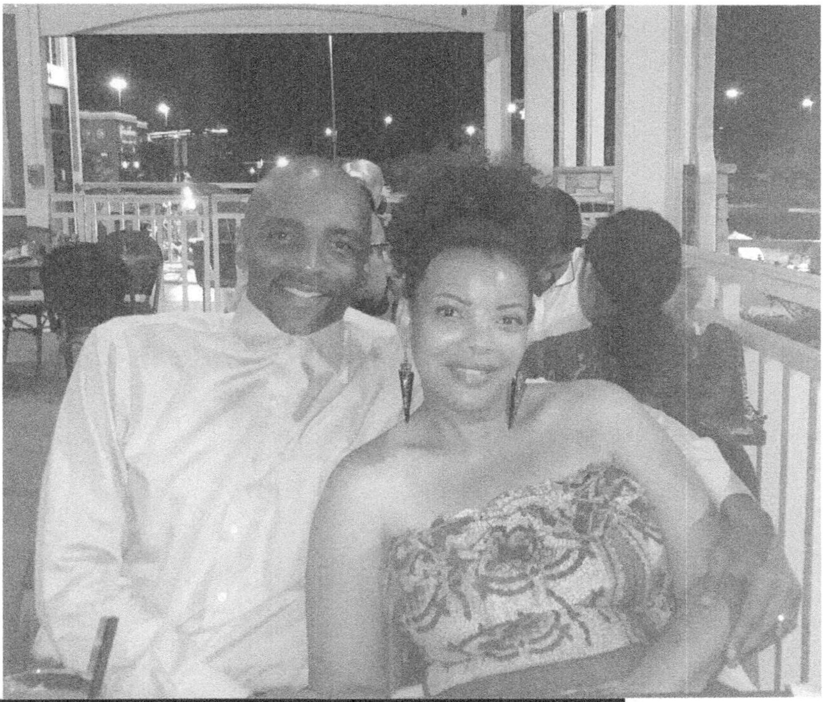

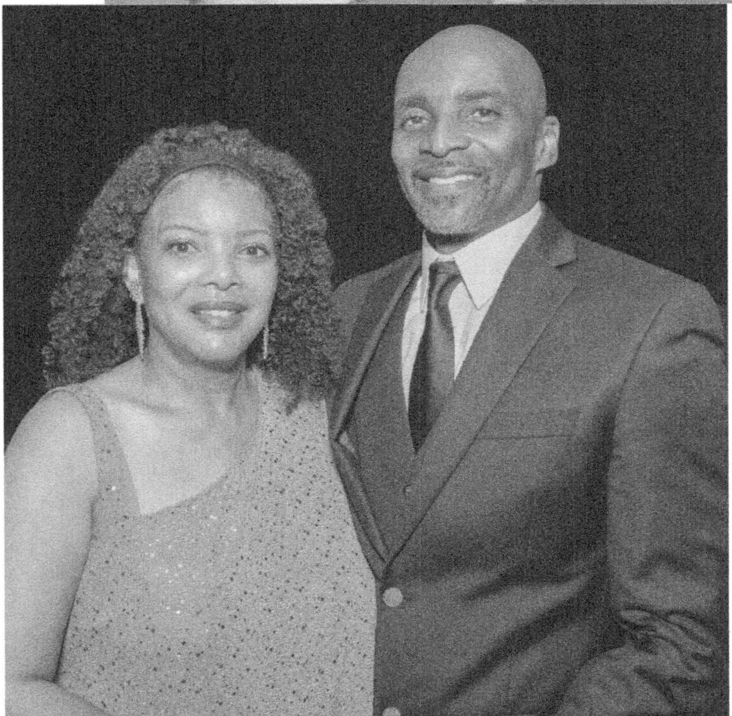

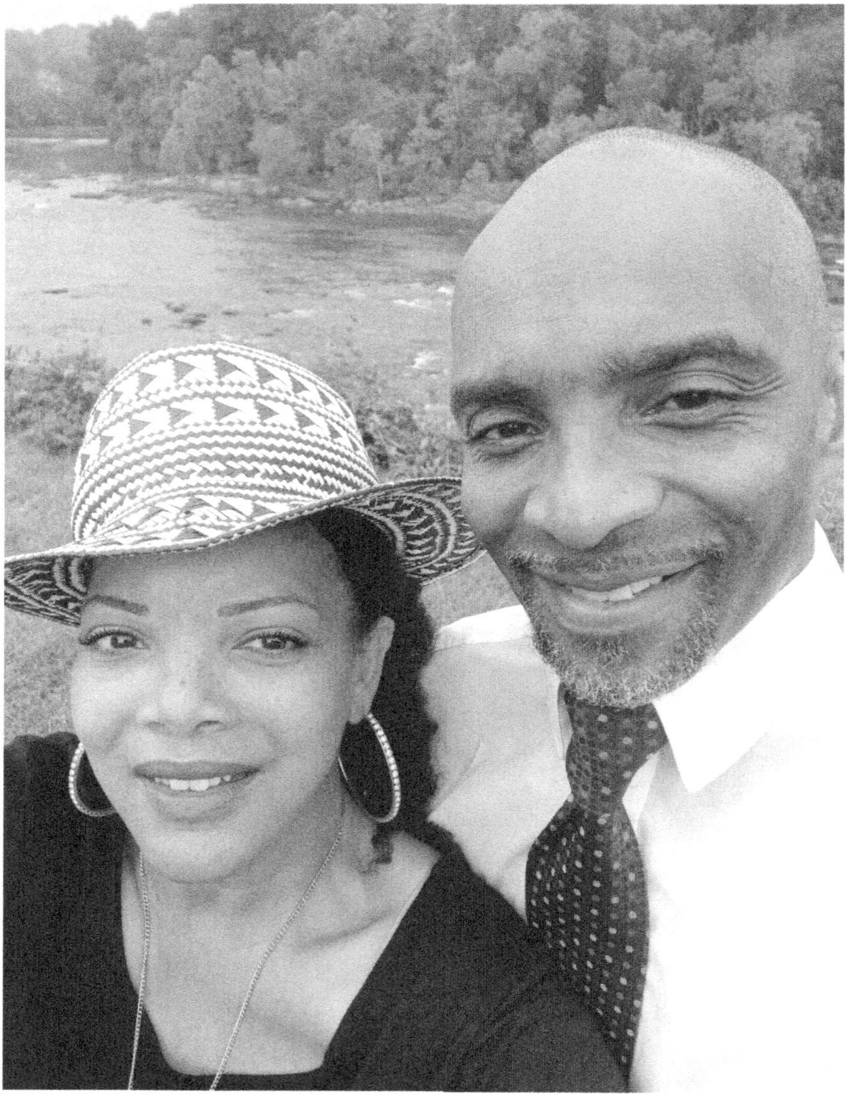

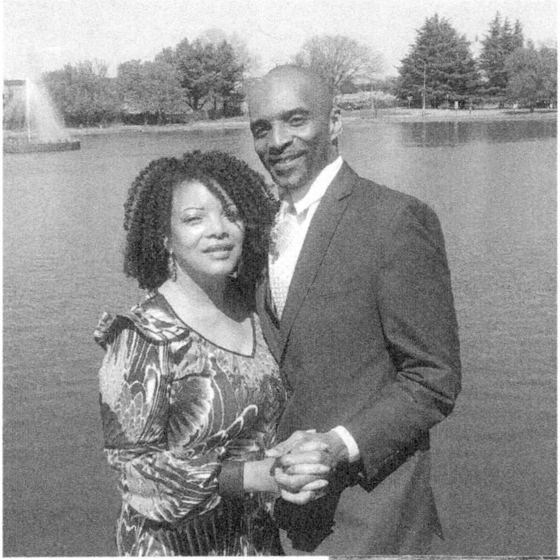
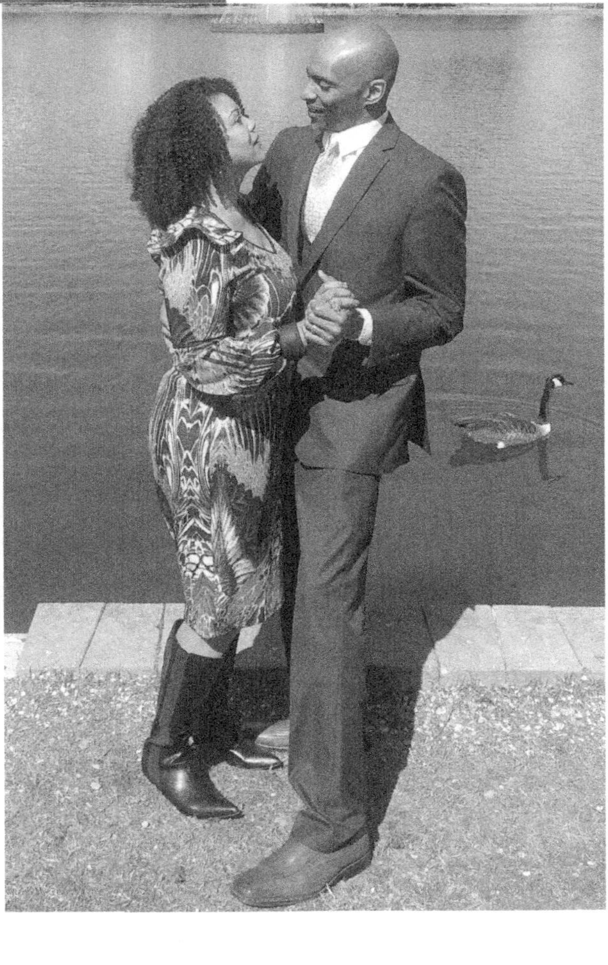

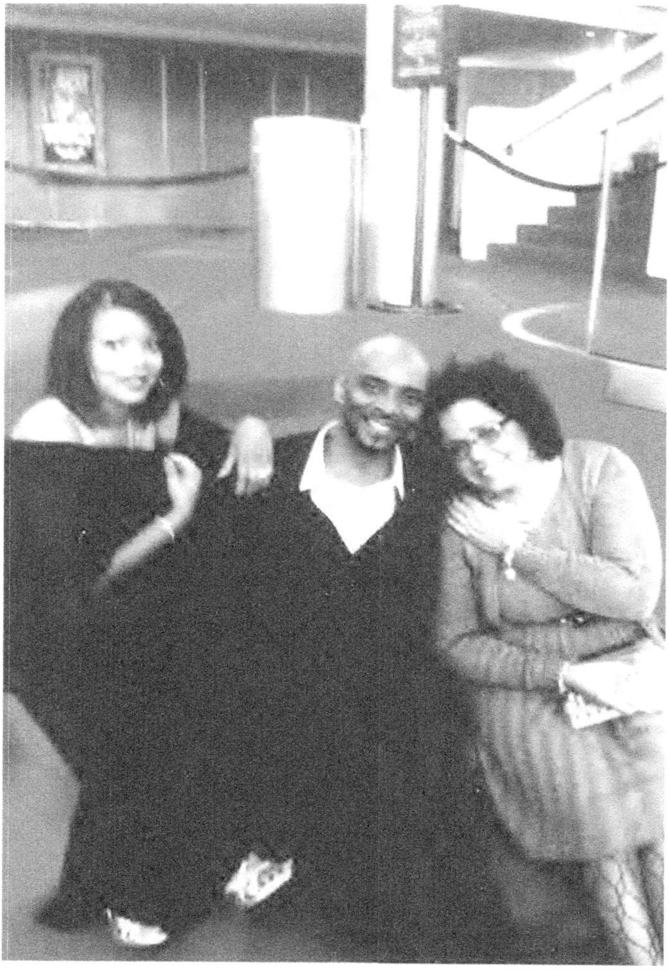

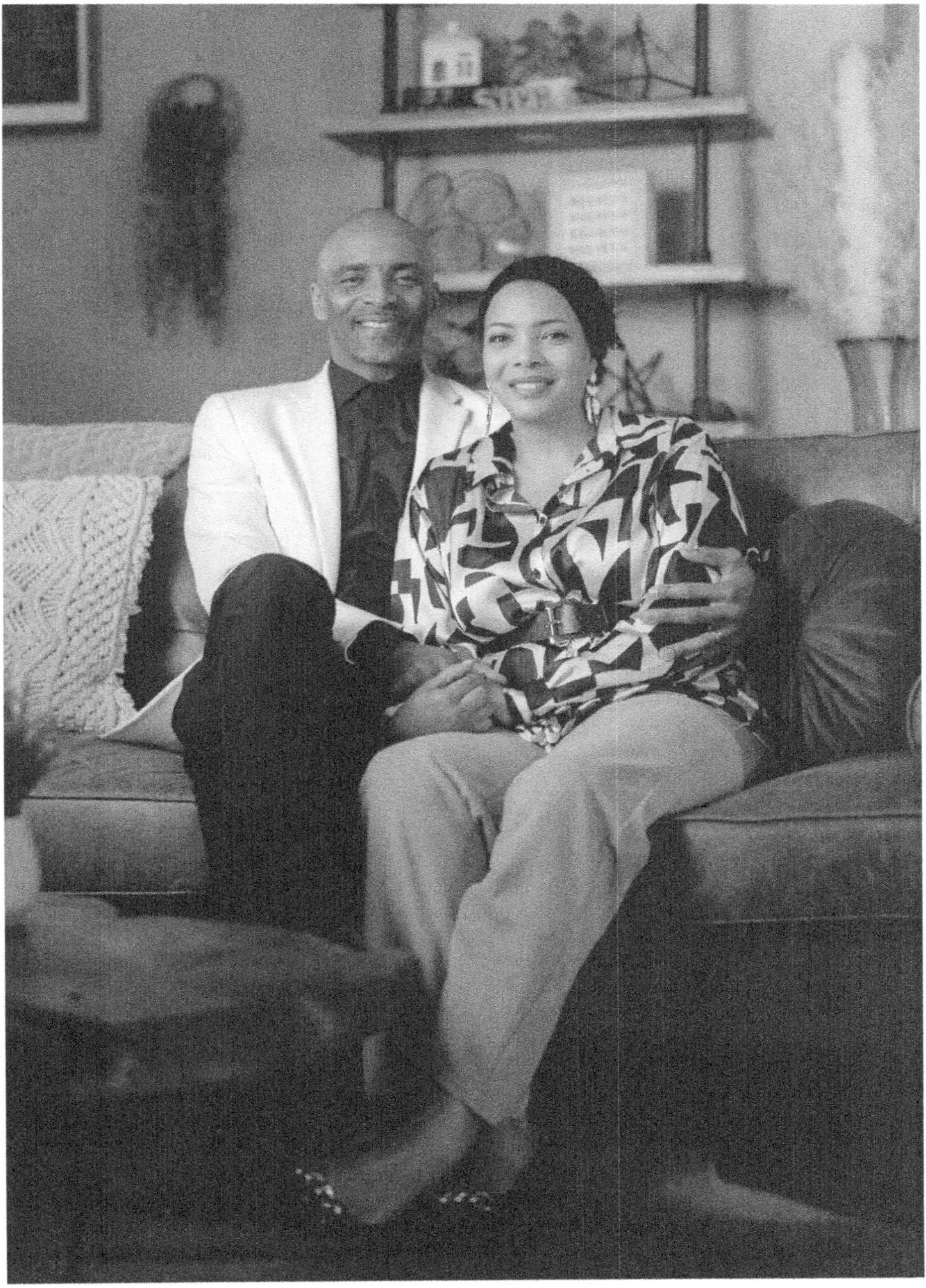

CHAPTER 16

UNEQUALLY YOKED

If there was one thing that proved to be a struggle in my new walk, it was the desire for female companionship. The desire for the club and secular music had vanished. I still danced and admired the gifting of others, but now my dancing was by myself and to music that glorified God. Yet, the desire for physical intimacy was more stubborn to relinquish its grip on me than I expected.

Even though I was not on the streets as before, there were two more relationships that I had no business taking part in. From reading the Word of God, I knew casual intimacy was not God's best, and I wanted to give that area to Him as well. I told myself that the next time I slept with a woman would be the day I marry. I promised to only date women I could imagine being my wife and the mother of my children. She would be a woman who could teach our daughter how to be a God-fearing woman and to show to a son the qualities of a virtuous wife. I thought I was some kind of spiritual superman who could be alone with an attractive woman. Unfortunately, impatience and poor decisions led to compromising situations where I settled for something else.

Inside, I was struggling with being alone. I had gotten used to the comfort and pleasure of sleeping beside a woman, and my body yearned to be held. I didn't want to displease God by sleeping with someone outside of marriage, but how long would I have to wait for God to hook me up with my future wife, one or two years, maybe five? Just the thought of it possibly being that long discouraged me.

Soft enticing touches, hugs, and kisses were not only wrong; they set me up for failure, where I went beyond God's limits. Again, this was not the plan I envisioned. A few years prior, I ended a relationship by refusing to have sex. But now, I was remorsefully and tearfully repenting as I dealt with constant harassment from Satan whispering "hypocrite."

The emotional and physical investment I gave to the relationships also made it hard to let go. Heartache made it hard to sleep and eat like I should, and faulty thinking told me only women struggle with heartache like this, so I viewed myself as a weak man. I went through stages of wondering what my former girlfriends were doing, who they might be with, and who might be touching them.

FAULTY THINKING TOLD ME ONLY WOMEN STRUGGLE WITH HEARTACHE LIKE THIS, SO I VIEWED MYSELF AS A WEAK MAN.

While dealing with my own hurt, I understood how couples argue and even threaten to harm one another. After connecting so deeply, you feel you have been played and some of your most intimate of secrets taken. You dread the possibility of your trust being betrayed. I understood that when sexual intimacy occurs, regardless of whether they are married, two people really do become one.

When they abruptly let go or leave, it feels like a piece of you is missing. These experiences led to such withdrawals that I felt like I was going out of my mind. At the same time, those thoughts produced clarity. This is why God set boundaries of intimacy between men and women. We weren't built to handle this kind of power without being surrendered to His authority.

In time, I eventually overcame the pain and grew more resolute to not repeat the same mistakes. Those relationships exposed my weakness and immaturity as well as theirs. As experienced before, my desire to run from the world showed to be stronger than the hold the world had on my girlfriend. They liked having a boyfriend who didn't want to club and who was yearning to be more like Christ, but not the persecution that arose from family and friends from being in such a relationship. This brought up an inner tension within them that seemed to birth resentment and frustration because of the Word of God.

WANTING THE BLESSING OF GOD IS ONE THING, BUT DYING TO SELF AND LETTING GO OF THE WORLD IS ANOTHER.

Wanting the blessing of God is one thing, but dying to self and letting go of the world is another. The rush to quench the feelings of loneliness and desire for intimacy set us up for failure. Going to church and using church clichés and language doesn't mean one was ready to live out the life of the virtuous woman or a faithful man. I soon found out, however, that because one's dress and demeanor doesn't match the description of the virtuous woman, that it didn't mean a person doesn't have a ready heart to do so.

> **GOING TO CHURCH AND USING CHURCH CLICHÉS AND LANGUAGE DOESN'T MEAN ONE WAS READY TO LIVE OUT THE LIFE OF THE VIRTUOUS WOMAN OR A FAITHFUL MAN.**

CHAPTER 17

SOMEONE WILL LIVE AND NOT DIE

The Stafford County Jail was one of the last places I thought I would ever be at the age of twenty-two, but there I was. I was nervous, and I had no idea what I was going to say, but I believed God had set up this job interview, so all I had to do was trust Him.

Several months before, I became frustrated with the pay I was earning at a local fast-food restaurant. I did some quick math as I swept the floor and realized it would take a while to save for a car or college tuition. I prayed for a different job and direction on where to look. Even though I knew it would take months of frustration before I found a better-paying job, I took strength from the Scriptures, and in remembering and believing that God's Word was true. God would provide, and in approximately two months, He provided me with an opportunity to be a deputy.

The thought of becoming a deputy sheriff seemed surreal. I always wanted to help people, but law enforcement never fit into any dream or vision of my life. Playing on NBA courts seemed more fitting for me than working in the county jail. Besides, as saved as I was, I still did not have a good feeling about law enforcement because of personal experience and reports of police brutality. But this was not the time to be picky, nor the time to complain about the way God was answering my prayer for a new job. He answered, and for that I was thankful.

After days of waiting and preparation, I was finally escorted to the back of the jail, where I became part of a subculture unlike any I had ever known. The first challenge was getting used to the distinct sound of a sliding jail door. The final clank declares that someone is being locked in or locked out, and done so with authority. I also had to get used to the cold, sinking apprehension as I drew closer to the housing area. Since I was a boy, stories of fights, stabbings, and rapes left a strong impression on me. From what I understood, this was a place where one could enter and possibly never come out.

We finally entered the catwalk and passed by the cells as the inmates studied the new person entering their world. I was nervous, but I fought hard not to show it, for fear was something inmates pick up on quickly.

Yet, the preeminent feeling that I had was not of fear, but excitement. My heart was full of eagerness and hope to share God and change lives. Behind these cell doors was a true mission field. Sadly, many of those men looked like me.

I was sad for every man I met behind bars, but those who resembled me disproportionally outnumbered the others. This was true not only in this county jail, but throughout the country.

Though I was only one person, I believed if I could just help somebody, that he would in return help another. As I worked as a sheriff's jailer, I learned about the inmates' childhood and faith—or lack thereof. Some were deeply knowledgeable about their faith, while others were agnostic.

As expected, men from all religions asked questions about what I believed and why I believed it, but many came intending to attack Christianity. Each question intended to challenge or discredit Christianity and the Bible only made me study and research more. Their questions made my faith grow and prepared me to defend my faith better.

Yet, I also understood that the most effective way to defend my faith was through my conduct. I knew my life would speak louder than my words. My generation listened more to what a person did than what one said. We could listen better once we perceived how much somebody cared.

I met many men during my time as a deputy sheriff, and most inmates had similar stories. Many came from broken homes where their father's absence left a serious void in their heart. Some wanted to know their dad, while others never wanted to see him for fear of what they might do. I learned that regardless of race, the longing to know or be close to our father is something we all have in common.

REGARDLESS OF RACE, THE LONGING TO KNOW OR BE CLOSE TO OUR FATHER IS SOMETHING WE ALL HAVE IN COMMON.

Another commonality was that most men talked about some type of Christian upbringing or influence in their lives, typically a faithful mother or grandparent who prayerfully gave them hope and faith in the Gospel. This faith was shown not just by teaching them, but by walking it out before them. Sadly, most of them turned away from God following the hypocrisy of an individual or congregation.

I also had to deal with harassment from some black inmates who said I was "a white man's nigger." To them, I was a traitor who worked for an organization they believed unjustly targeted, harassed, abused, and killed black men. Their insults irritated me, but I tried not to take it personally. I understood because I suffered disrespect and humiliation from law enforcement before I worked as a deputy. The first time I was provoked by an officer left me feeling violated and angry. Ironically, the offender became one of my supervisors after I got hired. The crazy thing is, I don't think he ever recognized me.

Nothing made that perspective clearer than the day of the verdict involving the officers tried in the Rodney King beating in 1992. When I heard the verdict of "not guilty," I froze in disbelief. Here I was a black man, standing in a uniform like those who were acquitted, trying to manage the rage fuming on the inside. "This is bull crap," I said to myself. Even the white colleague who shared the news said he was waiting for LA to explode.

But for me, I knew LA would burn that night. I thought if a guy as sheltered and levelheaded as myself could feel such disgust and fury, I could only imagine the emotions of LA residents who endured decades of racism, police brutality, and hopelessness. I shared this anguish with the black inmates who judged me in uniform before getting to know me.

My goal was to show black men that my position was for their good, not to betray our people, but to uplift them. First, I had to show it through my conduct and by acknowledging the injustice that was prevalent in our society. I built a rapport through genuine honesty and sincerity. I witnessed the tears in the eyes of the men and their families when I had to interrupt their visits to take them back to the cell block. I wanted them to know it grieved me as if it were my family, too. The pain transcended race, for I felt it for all.

The inmates knew I meant it when I told them I cared about their soul, and they took me seriously when I explained that faulty thinking was destroying them.

I just knew I had to witness to everyone—white or black, rich or poor, those who committed petty crimes and those whose crimes were horrific. They all needed the Lord and to know that no matter what they had done or how depraved the crime, they were loved by God, and they could be saved and have a relationship with the Lord.

This was real intervention and rehabilitation; everything else was a bandage on a bullet wound. It brought joy to my soul every time I learned something I said encouraged and uplifted another man. Feelings of purpose filled me whenever the Lord used me to lead someone in prayer to surrender their life and confess Jesus as Lord.

One man told me he was contemplating suicide, but was so encouraged and strengthened when he overheard a conversation between me and another inmate that he changed his mind. Another day, a white inmate asked if I was a preacher or a minister. I quickly replied, "No, I'm just a Christian."

"Well," he said, "you should be one, because I learned more from you than from my preacher back home."

God revealed three things to me through the souls and testimonies of these young men. First, I saw how mighty He is to use someone as inadequate and unworthy as me to bring life to others. It wasn't about having a degree or seminary training, not that they aren't important or needed. It is about knowing God's heart and having a willingness to seek and save those who don't know Him.

Second, He helped me see that Christianity in America has been watered down to such a level that many assume only a licensed minister or pastor does the most basic things that all Christians are supposed to say and do. Was this how far the standard had fallen?

Third, I discovered there is no greater joy than to be used to win souls for Christ. Within the year, I would be married. A year after that, I would watch the birth of my newborn son in 1993, but nothing could equal the joy and sense of purpose that flooded my soul when a soul got saved. No athletic achievement or fulfilled sexual fantasy could compare to seeing the initial and continued change in a life free from the emotional, mental, physical, and spiritual slavery of this troubled world.

CHAPTER 18

CAROLYN—

FOREVER MY LADY

While walking from the basketball court in Olde Forge, with my white tee and Michigan hat on, a red car slowly passed me. I smiled and waved, realizing that not only did I know the driver, but I recognized the passenger as well, an exceptionally beautiful young woman with an unforgettable face that I had met weeks before.

At that time, her outward appearance and persona did not indicate that church or the things of God were on her mind, which was enough to convince me to stay away.

Later, I was walking home from the neighborhood court and saw her again. She was sitting on the steps of her home, and I had to walk right past her. My intent was to smile, wave, maybe say hi, and keep it moving. That all changed when I heard a sweet voice calling, "Hey, come here."

"Lord, please help me," I said to myself, knowing I truly needed His help to resist getting caught up by her beauty. "Man, this can't be happening," I thought. But it was.

I walked over, trying to pretend I wasn't impressed, though inside I was feeling rather giddy. (Yea, I said giddy). After a few minutes of chatting, I was surprised to discover that we had several things in common. We both lived in the Northern Neck around the same time, and she had attended Lancaster High School—my old rival school. Go figure.

"It's a small world," we laughed as we found out how many mutual friends we had, which only made us more curious about each other. After the typical woman's interrogation, Carolyn was astonished and a little skeptical to learn that I didn't club, smoke, or drink, that I had no children, I was going to church regularly, and I was single.

The more we talked, the more I realized that beyond her short miniskirt, cigarette, and the beer in her hands, Carolyn was a woman with strong spiritual roots. She shared how she grew in a Holiness church and how her late father was a strong spiritual influence. She described church life as a child, her rebelliousness as a youth, and her desire to embrace those values again.

A seriousness flowed from her voice and showed on her face. Even though her father was deceased, his spiritual influence was very present in her heart and mind. The more I talked about spiritual things, the more she confessed I reminded her of her father. She continued to share her determination to leave the streets. Going back to church with her daughter was priority number one.

Hearing this warmed my heart and rearranged my thinking. Carolyn's sincerity and substance made me see her as a potential wife. Truth be told, just her looks caught my attention, but I knew she needed time to walk out her new priorities. There was no future in dating if she remained the same. Casual friends would be all that we could be, I gently told her, hoping she would return to her faith, not for me, but because it was God's desire. Our days of talking turned into weeks and as time passed, she gave up drinking, smoking, and those miniskirts. WHEW! (Sorry. I had a flashback.)

We grew closer through a weekly routine of Bible study dates and watching my favorite TV ministry together. However, spending time alone outside of Bible study led us to yielding to our flesh, which I found hard to control once I let it loose again. The beauty was that Carolyn's growth in the Lord helped, especially when she saw how it grieved me each time we crossed God's boundaries. Carolyn became the stronger one, resisting my advances while reminding me of things I said that strengthened her.

This was the kind of woman I needed. This was the selfless kind of love that would protect and not hurt me. Inside, I truly sensed that she was the one. Mother confirmed it when she said, "I have a peace about her."

MOTHER CONFIRMED IT WHEN SHE SAID, "I HAVE A PEACE ABOUT HER."

Mother's words sealed it for me as confirmation from God. Though Mother sometimes said things that were way off base, many times her words were derived from her spirit and connected with mine—whether or not her observation was in my favor. This time, it happened to be in my favor.

About a month later, Carolyn and I were engaged, and several months later, she became Carolyn Monica Carey, and forever my lady. Though upcoming years would show that we should have taken more time to grow in the Lord individually, to prepare financially, and to be healed in certain areas in our lives, I knew that I was blessed of the Lord to have a gift like her.

CHAPTER 19

GROWTH AND REFLECTION

The year 1993 brought joy and happiness, along with an expectation of much more to come. I had a good job and a beautiful wife and daughter. Carolyn and I also had a newborn son, Antwaun Jr. He was born eleven days before our first wedding anniversary, which made it a memorable and precious time. I felt so blessed to see God's faithfulness as He did what He said He would do.

I could have been in the streets, in the wrong relationship, dead, or in prison, but I wasn't. My story could have been so different. Only by God's grace and mercy (underserved kindness) did I make it out, and now was the time to share of His power to change a life. As I continued to witness about Him in and outside of the jail, I understood more and I became bolder. I continued learning from the questions people asked me concerning Christianity. Between the two missionary fields, I gained a depth of knowledge and experience beyond what some seminaries could offer alone. This was on-the-job training instructed by the Holy Spirit.

My dreams of playing in the NBA or overseas weakened considerably during this time. Though I still believed it was possible, significant injuries impacted my athletic abilities. It became harder to play at the level necessary for a professional team to consider taking a chance on a relatively unknown player.

I played and worked out as though a miracle could happen, but I knew it would be just that, a miracle. With my new perspective about what really brings happiness, I could handle the disappointment of that dream not coming true. However, I still had an inordinate love for the game.

My competitive spirit was a stronghold, and I struggled to overcome the desire to prove myself. I became addicted to training and playing in the streets or in men's leagues, and the need to prove to others that I could have made in the NBA was a hindrance to my Christian walk.

When temptation with women came my way, the Spirit of God strengthened me to walk away through daily habits of prayer, study, and focus on His Word. I was thrilled to be an example to show other men how to love God and be faithful to their wives.

I WAS THRILLED TO BE AN EXAMPLE TO SHOW MEN HOW TO LOVE GOD AND BE FAITHFUL TO THEIR WIVES.

I had need of no one else, for I was truly blessed with a beautiful woman of God. For me, there was nothing and no one that could make me forfeit my testimony or my wife's trust. I knew other strong men who had fallen but it wouldn't happen to me.

While believing and declaring is good, it must come with humility and a true understanding of the fact that though we may feel strong, we must never underestimate the unyielding pull of the flesh or the subtle deceit of the devil. According to Proverbs 4:23 (KJV) and 1 Corinthians 10:12 (KJV), one must truly guard his or her heart with all diligence and take heed lest one fall.

WE MUST NEVER UNDERESTIMATE THE UNYIELDING PULL OF THE FLESH OR THE SUBTLE DECEIT OF THE DEVIL.

CHAPTER 20

THE DEADLY INCEPTION

I was on the night shift as I went through my nightly Bible reading and pushups. Weeknights were slow, which made for a long night of trying to stay awake, so after checking on the inmates, I immersed myself in the Bible, stopping only to work out or get something to eat or drink. It was a great way to stay awake while I strengthened myself spiritually and physically, which made the time valuable and precious.

Many nights, a certain supervisor asked me to relieve him for smoke breaks and to get snacks from the kitchen. One night, he seemed to request my help more than normal. Slightly irritated, I casually complained to one of my partners about having to relieve him so often. My partner informed me the supervisor wasn't just smoking and eating. He was watching the Playboy channel.

"There's no Playboy channel on our TV!" I argued.

"Yes, there is," he insisted.

He explained that even though the channel was supposed to be scrambled, somehow the audio came through, and sometimes even the picture was viewable. I thought my partner was just trying to be funny, so I repeatedly told him to stop playing with me, but he maintained his claim was true.

I thought nothing of it until the next time I went to the kitchen to get a snack and catch up on the news and sports highlights. The moment I felt tempted inside my heart quickly cautioned, "Don't do it!"

I knew the convicting voice was trying to keep me from doing anything that wasn't pleasing to God, but the voice of curiosity kept saying, "Just look to see if it's true. If something crazy comes on, just turn from it, simple as that."

Turning the channel was easy but turning away from it was not that simple. At first, there was nothing but a scrambled screen. Then suddenly, I heard a woman having sex. The sound of her voice captivated me and instantly took me back to younger days. I felt ashamed immediately, and though unlikely, I feared someone may walk in on me.

I turned away from the television, only to turn back again. Curiosity had just introduced me to one of the worst enemies of my life.

I stayed free from any form of porn until this time, except for a brief exposure to a film and a few sneak peeks at somebody else's Playboy magazines during my preteen and early teenage years. I was ignorant of the seeds even those quick glances had planted, but now porn had found me, or I had found it.

I allowed curiosity to unlock the door to a new world. Despite my regret, I felt like my mind and heart instantly acquired a virus. Many nights at home, I entertained the fantasy and repented afterward, only to return to it again.

As time went on, my curiosity and cravings grew. Before this unwanted inception, I wouldn't watch R-rated or even some PG-rated movies. I was determined to keep my mind renewed, my spirit strong, and my home free from anything that would defile it. I wanted my home to be a place where, if Jesus were to walk through my house, He would find nothing that would grieve Him.

AS TIME WENT ON, MY CURIOSITY AND CRAVINGS GREW.

But now I was addicted to the erotic rush provided by the porn channels. I used stall tactics to avoid coming to bed until Carolyn fell asleep waiting for me. Once I knew she was sleeping, I turned to the desired station. I kept the volume low so that I could entertain my eyes without awakening her. If I suspected she may wake up, I quickly changed the channel to a basketball game and turned up the volume.

Eventually, my obsession grew, and the scrambled stations were not enough. Unknown to Carolyn, I rented R-rated movies I knew included explicit scenes. The more I watched these sinful fantasies, the more I felt like something inside of me was dying. Even though I couldn't see the impact porn had on me right away, the consequences would be clearly exposed in time.

What was I doing?! I constantly scolded myself, "You have a gorgeous woman, but you choose to spend time with an actress on a screen. This does not make sense!" Yet, amid this dark place, I had a puzzling revelation, especially when I started spending money to feed my lust. In the past, I wondered how addicts could do the most irrational things to purchase their drug of choice. How could a person give their body away? How could one offer up their daughter, rob their mother, or spend up to their entire paycheck for a little piece of rock? I never condemned them in my heart, thank God, but I still could not comprehend the why or the how. But now I knew.

Here I was in the early stages of an addiction that consumed my thoughts and altered my behavior. I gave into the force, despite the shame and guilt it brought me afterward. I hid my addiction from the world, and I felt like a hypocrite.

Where could I go? Who could I talk to? I never heard a pastor or leader talk about porn addiction, or any other sexual issues for that matter, and I couldn't think of anyone to confide in about such a personal and embarrassing problem. I was isolated and alone.

At the time, I had no idea how many American men were addicted to porn. I didn't know how many professing Christian men and leaders struggled just like me. Nor did I know the brain released the same chemicals in both porn addiction and drug use.

Last, I didn't know the generational propensity toward such a thing. Some people call it a curse. Perhaps the enemy of my soul believed he had a right to entice me, just as he had with other men in my family.

Though I would gain victories over this stronghold for a period of weeks or even months, it would find its way back into my life, each time with increasing intensity. I was determined to defeat my addiction alone, even though it was harder to overcome each time. This foolish thinking would prove disastrous in years to come. In the not-too-distant future, this fatal attraction would cause one of the biggest regrets of my life.

IN THE NOT-TO-DISTANT FUTURE, THIS FATAL ATTRACTION WOULD CAUSE ONE OF THE BIGGEST REGRETS OF MY LIFE.

CHAPTER 21

THE MOVE

It was the fall of 1995, and like a revolving door, I was back in the Northern Neck to start a new chapter in my life. This time I returned with a purpose and a beautiful family. I left the sheriff's department for the potential of advancement at another facility in Virginia. We moved into a home passed on to my grandmother from her sister. The low mortgage gave us hope of possibly becoming homeowners in the future. It was a one-bedroom home with no air conditioning and only an oil stove to heat the house in the winter. We believed it would be a wise investment, so we were more than willing to humble ourselves for a while. I had immaculate credit and a plan to have my family in a good financial position in five years.

What better scenario to raise my young children than in the country area near my grandparents and my wife's family! With a nice front yard to play in, a gentle country breeze coming through the window at night, and the smell of Grandma and Granddaddy's breakfast on Saturday mornings, it would be the bomb for my little ones and for Carolyn and me. This place was full of my best childhood memories, and I wanted the same wonderful experiences for my kids.

We soon connected with Mother's (the Martin family's) local church where I attended when I lived with Grandma. I left as an adolescent that caused trouble and fell asleep during "moments of meditation" in the back pews, but I returned as a young man on fire for God, eager to praise and testify, and ready to be an example to the youth and young adults. The beautiful white church on the hill would soon become dearer to me than I could imagine, but first it was time to start my new job and build a promising career.

I LEFT AS AN ADOLESCENT THAT CAUSED TROUBLE AND FELL ASLEEP DURING "MOMENTS OF MEDITATION" IN THE BACK PEWS, BUT I RETURNED AS A YOUNG MAN ON FIRE FOR GOD, EAGER TO PRAISE AND TESTIFY, AND READY TO BE AN EXAMPLE TO THE YOUTH AND YOUNG ADULTS.

CHAPTER 22

THE COLDEST ENCOUNTER

The time had finally come. After a few weeks, I began my new job excited for the opportunity to advance at a new facility. Knowledge and experience from the academy and from the staff and inmates in Stafford all prepared me for this new position. I believed great things lie ahead for me and my amazing new wife. Instead, my career took a turn for the worse, and in a short period of time.

I worked the night shift on my third day at the new job. After I arrived on that unforgettable evening, I waited patiently in the control room for my assignment. The shift change had already occurred for the night, so I wondered where my supervisor was. I knew I had a big area to cover, so I did not want to be late for safety checks. I learned from experience that inmates knew when shift changes occurred and they became familiar with each officer's check patterns. A lot of detrimental, and even deadly things can happen during the transition.

At my previous job, an inmate would have laid on the floor with a broken jaw for hours if I had not made the safety check at the appropriate time. He claimed he fell from his bunk, but it was more likely his roommate had assaulted him and he was now pretending to be asleep. On another occasion, I saved an inmate who slit his wrist. The other inmates said blood shot from his wrist like a fountain. By the time I arrived, there was a pool of blood approximately 20 feet from where I found him. Had I come fifteen minutes later, who knows what might've happened?

I knew it was critical that rounds were made on schedule, so I was concerned when a substantial amount of time passed with no sign of my supervisor. He finally arrived in the control room with no sense of urgency, and he gave me my assignment. He told me to cover all the units for the night, which took at least fifteen to twenty minutes.

As I made my initial round, I received orders to get an inmate and to escort him to medical. I radioed back to advise my supervisor that I had not finished my rounds, but I got a stern response that escorting the inmate to the nurse was priority. Not wanting to appear resistive, I followed orders. I took the inmate to the nurse, waited until the visit was finished, and then escorted him back to his unit.

The scheduled safety checks were now way past the mandatory time. I returned to finish my initial round before proceeding to the max unit. I was not yet familiar with the inmates' specific charges, but I knew the max unit was for inmates who were violent, suicidal, or a serious flight risk.

As I approached the first floor, I glanced at the log sheet and noticed that almost an hour had passed since the last check in the max unit. I sighed in frustration. "This was avoidable," I thought.

My supervisor expected me to initial the log sheet to signify rounds were done on schedule, which put me in an awkward position—and it wasn't the first time. Two nights before, I notified the same supervisor when I found the log sheets were missing signatures. When I brought it to his attention, his only response was something like, "Yeah, that should've been done."

When I looked at him with confusion, he told me to get the log sheet caught up. Reluctantly, I signed the log sheet because I did not want my supervisor or other officers to think that I wasn't a "team player," especially over something that could be considered minor.

Now, not only was I late for my own rounds, but I faced signing off on another officer's safety checks again. Though annoyed, I signed the bottom sheets, determined to let my supervisor know that this would be the last time I would cover for someone else's missed rounds, no matter how minor it may seem.

After signing, I walked to the upper floor of the max unit to check on the rest of the inmates. As I looked through one of the cell windows, I saw a perplexing scene I will never forget, no matter how hard I try.

The inmate was up against the wall with his eyes wide open and his neck tilted slightly to the side. At first, I thought he was playing around or conducting some weird meditation. I called out to get his attention, but he did not respond. Just as I was about to call his name again, I noticed his feet not touching the floor.

The sight caused the most surreal, breath-taking fear. Was he hanging, or was this one of the most ingenious escape tricks I had ever seen? I called on the radio for the door to open. I braced myself in anticipation of a sudden attack.

My fight-or-flight response took over like never before. By the time the door was open a few moments later, I was focused and ready to kill if I had to. I called again, but no answer. I still expected a set-up. Is this sheet around his neck really happening? Could he still possibly stand on his tiptoes?

Abruptly, a heightened sense of awareness within me registered the tangible presence of death. Approximately twenty seconds had passed since I first saw him through the cell window. I stared at the man's face nervously as the eerie stillness of his eyes confirmed this was no trick. The contorted look on his face spoke directly to my soul, "I am not here. By the powers of pain and fear, I have left." Except for a few funerals, this was my first experience with a corpse, and it messed with my mind.

The lieutenant rushed in and stopped in his tracks as he realized what had happened. Together, we took the man down and laid him on the floor. We faced each other, kneeling on opposite sides of him, and looked at one another as if to say, "What are you going to do?"

During my brief career, I was assaulted by an inmate, and I'd been in other extremely stressful situations, but this was my first potential inmate suicide. I became increasingly anxious as I waited for instruction and leadership from the lieutenant. Much to my despair, he appeared consumed with dread. Suddenly, I understood his unspoken orders, "I expect you to perform CPR."

Time was ticking, and I didn't know how to tell the lieutenant he was more qualified to do CPR than me. What I did know was that this was somebody's son, or brother, or maybe some child's father. If it were my family member, I would expect and hope the authorities responsible for my loved one would do their job.

All my life, I enjoyed the warmth of a woman's lips, but suddenly I found myself mouth-to-mouth with a dead man. I tried not to gag as I breathed into his mouth. Still not convinced this wasn't a morbid escape plot, I gave one cycle of CPR after another while praying he wouldn't bite me.

The rescue breaths and chest compressions accomplished nothing, but I continued until other officers arrived. I answered questions and then drifted out of the way until the rescue squad and state troopers took over. Then I retreated to the nearby staircase to catch my breath. Though still surrounded by medical personnel and police, I never felt so confused and alone. I spit every time I thought of where my mouth had been, and I kept thinking, "This is not happening to me."

I glanced up and noticed the superintendent studying the log sheets with my supervisor. Suddenly, it dawned on me that I never signed the inmate's log sheet. I perceived the superintendent noticed how much time was unaccounted for and when the lapse started. Then, my supervisor received the log sheets from the superintendant and walked straight to me. He held the clipboard toward me and stated, "This needs to be caught up."

For a few seconds, I stood there staring at him in disbelief that the superintendent condoned, even asked, that I falsify the log sheet of an inmate who had likely been dead for more than an hour. "You know I'm not responsible for some of those times," I stated. He just looked at me as though he had never heard me and extended the log sheets and pen closer to my midsection. Fearful and intimidated by the seriousness of the situation and the nonverbal approval of the superintendent, I signed the log sheet— something I would soon regret.

When the state police questioned me, I told them the truth about everything, including that I caught up the log sheets for missed rounds. My supervisor told me to go home early, so I left stunned, wondering why this was happening to me.

When I arrived home and told Carolyn, she just held me. I continued spitting even though I washed my mouth out thoroughly. I just could not shake that my mouth had been on a dead man.

When I returned to work, my supervisor was different. He was on-point with his duties, and he had an attitude. The ongoing investigation could cause job loss or a lawsuit for negligence or for the cover-up.

In the next few days, I reviewed the standard of operating procedures for the facility and learned two people were required to do checks in the max unit. I never should have been asked or allowed to go in there by myself. I also met with an officer from internal affairs for questioning. He said he had worked at the same sheriff's office in Stafford where I came from. He heard a lot of good things about me, including that the officers described me as a sincere Christian.

I told him everything I knew about the incident. He stated he could tell something was wrong with the other stories, but he never elaborated on what that was. The look on his face told me I had just put him in an uncomfortable position, but he said he believed I was truthful, so I left feeling like everything would be ok.

I never saw the internal affairs officer again. Within a week of the inmate's death, I was placed on paid administrative leave while the investigation continued. A few days later, I shook my head in shock as I read the newspaper report that there were no signs of foul play or negligence. I spent my time on leave battling a torrent of conflicting emotions. The cover-up baffled me, but I was relieved it seemed I would keep my job. Mostly, I felt awful that this man's family may never know the truth about the negligence involved in their loved one's death.

One day, I received a letter to come to the facility for a meeting. It caught me off guard, and I thought it was strange, but I did not suspect anything was amiss. However, as soon as I arrived at the meeting, I knew I was truly unprepared for a very serious meeting.

When I walked into the meeting, two sheriffs from surrounding counties, two lawyers, and four colleagues were waiting for me. Every officer involved in the night of the hanging came with representation, except me. The first lawyer was with the officer who worked in the control room. The other lawyer represented the facility on behalf of the superintendent, my immediate supervisor, and the lieutenant who helped me take the inmate down. A sinking feeling came over me as I realized I was neither made privy nor prepared for what was about to happen. Everyone asked me questions, yet no one would answer mine. My colleagues either made false accusations toward me or took my statements out of context. When the lawyers shielded the officers from responding to me, I knew this was a set-up.

According to the lawyer, my supervisor claimed he had assigned me to my area as soon as I came to work, but I just didn't go.

"That's not true!" I argued. "If I blatantly disobeyed orders for thirty minutes, then why didn't you reprimand me?" There was no answer, and I knew it was simply my word against his.

One of the sheriffs from a neighboring county said he was puzzled by my statement that I didn't finish my checks in the max unit, because the logbooks in the control room stated we did complete the checks that night.

I explained, "Apparently, the officer in the control room signed his logbooks to cover himself and/or me. If I wanted to lie to cover myself, all I had to do was to sign the log sheet on the cell door and both logs would have covered me."

Again, there was no reply, and I understood this meeting was not about looking for the truth. It was about closure for their dilemma because my story could of caused a major lawsuit and many officers would lose their jobs, including the superintendent.

My gut sank as I finally realized I was their scapegoat. How naive I was to think the authorities would risk their jobs or a lawsuit over the truth. My heart filled with rage. I wanted to burst out and call them all liars and cowards.

I felt a hangman's noose unjustly choking the life out of my career, my dreams, and my family's livelihood. I left the meeting feeling used and helpless in anticipation of their pre-determined verdict.

My termination notice came in the mail not long after the meeting. I had never been fired before in my life and the sting bruised my self-esteem hard. To make matters worse unemployment benefits were denied because I was fired

---

I FELT A HANGMAN'S NOOSE UNJUSTLY CHOKING THE LIFE OUT OF MY CAREER, MY DREAMS, AND MY FAMILY'S LIVELIHOOD.

for negligence. I appealed, only to watch the superintendent treat me like a criminal during the hearing. Thanks to him, I was denied any kind of assistance.

I left the appeal hearing disillusioned and livid, wondering if this was the kind of indignant fury that caused people to go on shooting sprees. I had never felt such a desire for vengeance. I was enraged with anyone who contributed to my demise by what was said or unsaid, but the weight of my anger was toward the superintendent whose manipulation led to my firing.

The wrongful firing opened my eyes to internal corruption in both the private sector and in local and federal governments. I didn't need statistics or episodes of 60 Minutes to know dishonesty and fraud were prevalent.

We live in a world where certain cliques protect their own at the expense of fairness and justice. Perpetrators camouflage the truth to make themselves look like victims, and victims look like perpetrators. In a world system where offenders in authority take what doesn't belong to them, men still get hung, both literally and figuratively, without the truth of their story ever being told.

This is the stuff they don't teach in schools. The curriculum doesn't include crooked or discriminatory practices, but I saw many situations similar to mine, cover-ups most people don't see.

Oh, to quote my brother Marvin, "It makes me wanna holler the way they do my life!"[vi]

CHAPTER 23

LUSTFUL GAMES

I fought a constant barrage of thoughts of revenge and unforgiveness toward the superintendent for months after I was fired. I thought about my young son and daughter, who were naive to the wickedness and complexities of living in this world. They had no clue how all their best efforts to be everything their teachers and parents hoped for could fail at the hands of politics and prejudice.

I wanted to draw major attention to the situation by contacting either the NAACP or a TV station in hopes of getting justice, but I chose not to because my own lack of integrity contributed to the situation. I also did not want it to consume any more of my time or hinder my ability to forgive.

With God's help, I let it go. It hurt my mind, heart, and livelihood, but I felt peace in my spirit. Though it appeared those involved got away, they didn't. God sees everything, and He will render His judgment when and how He sees fit. Revenge is His, not mine.

During this turbulent time, I struggled to provide for my family, but I was too proud to ask for help. As I looked for a new job, I relied on credit cards to pay for basic needs instead of taking advantage of food stamps or other assistance.

Proverb 16:18 proved to be true: "Pride goeth before destruction, and an haughty spirit before a fall." Proverbs 16:18 (KJV) My attempts to maintain a facade of normalcy came at a price. It wasn't long before we were so deep in debt that I had to file for bankruptcy.

I found moments of solace serving in the two areas I loved most, church and basketball. I worked with the youth in Sunday school and Bible study. Over time, people saw God's hand on me; however, I would learn later that a few others saw me as a source of irritation.

MY ATTEMPTS TO MAINTAIN A FACADE OF NORMALCY CAME AT A PRICE.

I also had the pleasure of coaching the Northumberland boys' junior varsity basketball team alongside my mentor, Coach Stevenson. Reconnecting and coaching alongside him was a delightful honor that also helped me cope. By January, I found a good job as the sports coordinator for the YMCA in Kilmarnock, Virginia. After just two months, I was blessed to transfer as the sports coordinator to the Recreation Department closer to home in Northumberland.

Even amid difficulty, I could see God's favor in my life. Through the challenges, I gained priceless insight that gave me a heart for justice and helped me grow as a minister. Although some areas in my heart were getting better, others were decaying. Even though I was coaching, teaching in the church, and mentoring youth, attacks from both outside myself and within led to another fall.

Rumors spread fast in a small, rural country area, and they can do serious damage. In just a short time, rumors spread that I had become a drug dealer, wife beater, and womanizer. It was not the first time I had ever heard rumors about me, but that was mostly before I centered my life in church. But now, attacks on me were spreading to family, work, and church.

The rumor that I beat Carolyn hurt me the most, and it bothered her even more. By the time I heard it, the rumor had spread through the school system and the churches and had found its way to my in-laws. The attack on my character, I assumed to some degree, hindered my ability to tell young men in the community about God.

I saw the ramifications when a boy from our youth basketball team blurted out a disturbing confession. After he shared how he was upset about a lie that was perpetrated about him, I shared how I also was the victim of malicious lies, including the lies that I beat my wife. I also shared how I felt like confronting the people who I believed were responsible, but that it was best to leave it in God's hands and not let it bother me.

Surprisingly, he confessed he heard the rumor from a young man I witnessed to. The young man said I was a cool dude, but that it was a shame that I beat my wife. In that moment, I realized how fast and far a lie could travel, and the damage it could do to everyone who hears or repeats it by shaping a false image of someone. Though my outward walk did not match these lies and rumors, inwardly I still gave place to the enemy. As I caved to temptation, one rumor would soon become a reality.

In my heart and behind the scenes, I entertained myself with pornography. The draw was dormant, but still there, so what started as an occasional slip soon increased in frequency. Little by little, my defenses weakened, making it harder to turn down sexual advances from women. Suddenly, I caught myself doing a double take when an attractive woman looked at me with interest.

I allowed glances to progress into flirting, which then turned into one of the worst moments of my life. Weeks of playing with fire and being overly confident that I could stop at any time set the stage for a complete fall. The drive home that night was a serious challenge through the downpour of tears as I pounded the steering wheel in outrage at myself.

God gave me so many opportunities to prevent this from happening. Previous close encounters should have been ample warnings that my resistance was weak. I should have learned that I wasn't strong enough to continue playing lustful games. As I drove home, all I could think about was how I had betrayed God and my wife. Although I had already done so, both in actions and in my heart, this seemed much worse.

The more I thought about how this would hurt Carolyn and how I had damaged my witness, the more the torment grew. I was so overwhelmed that I thought it would be better to die than to tell my wife what I had done. I would rather die than to be unable to declare my faithfulness to my wife, to declare "no" when someone asked if I'd betrayed my marriage. This was not the legacy I wanted to leave my children or the testimony I intended to reach others for Christ. The word hypocrite screamed in my mind, pressing me lower and lower.

I found the strength to tell Carolyn, who was understandably wounded by my confession. But she loved me so much that she forgave me without making me feel even worse about myself. She saw my suffering and regret and considered that, without my confessing, she would not have known. I believe she would have picked up quickly that something was wrong with me. My pain and regret would have shown when we prayed, worshipped in church, or when we were intimate. The guilt of knowing that I was living a lie would've been felt in my touch as well as discerned by my lack of boldness shown all over my face.

I just wanted to be real and right before God, Carolyn, and others. If that meant exposing myself, then so be it. Proverbs 28:13 states that "He that covereth his sins shall not prosper, but whoso confesseth and forsaketh them shall have mercy." Proverbs 28:13 (KJV) Mercy, undeserved forgiveness, is what I needed more than ever.

HE THAT COVERETH SINS SHALL NOT PROSPER, BUT WHOSO CONFESSETH AND FORSAKETH THEM SHALL HAVE MERCY. PROVERBS 28:13 (KJV)

CHAPTER 24

STANDING IN SILENT AWE

As I tried to leave the past behind, I came to grips with the truth that I had a strong propensity toward sexual sins. I learned that if I gave this area any attention, the desire would grow faster than any weed. I had to be intentional, continually and actively striving to stay focused on the things of God. Though I knew couldn't make up for my past, I also knew I could make the devil pay by growing and witnessing while exposing his evil ways and intentions.

I learned the church needed a male chaperone for an upcoming youth retreat. I always heard good things about the retreat when I was younger, but I never went, so when a retreat leader asked me to chaperone, I agreed to go.

I arrived excited for my opportunity to experience the event I heard so much about as a youth. I saw and experienced unusual things the first night when nearly five hundred youth from all over the region gathered in an auditorium to hear the Word of God.

As the Word of God was presented, I noticed a powerful shift in the atmosphere. Youth from our church who appeared indifferent and unmoved by services at home showed powerful displays of emotional stress and conviction, especially the women. All throughout the building, both young girls and older women alike let out hair-raising screams similar to a woman going through a difficult childbirth.

I stood in silent awe, at a total loss for words. Whatever was happening was beyond anyone's control, and there were clearly more people in need than ministers available to care for them. I did not know whether to just stand by or to carefully intervene. I felt so out of place, yet suddenly, I felt led to do something unfamiliar and uncomfortable, but I couldn't just stand there. I gently laid my hands on the backs of two youths and began praying. I didn't know even what to pray for, but I knew God would lead me. I just wanted the youth to be healed, and I trusted that if I ministered to them, God would do the rest. Their lives could then be changed by this moment, and I was glad I was there to witness it.

When things settled down, the youth had an opportunity to come on stage and share about what God had done for them before or during the service. As testimony time began, a young man I had prayed for walked on the stage. I was shocked to hear him testify that when I had prayed for him, I said exactly what he needed to hear. He then shared that he was rededicating his life back to God. I sat in my seat surprised and bewildered. I knew nothing about the boy, so how could I have spoken exactly what he needed to hear?

I'd laid hands on folks in prayer, and now this! My mind was blown. In that second, I felt led to go on stage and testify to encourage the youth. I shared how important it was to grow in the Lord and that the devil was out to kill, steal, and destroy their lives through pride, lust, and other sins.

As an example, I shared that my little brother could have been a stabbing victim over an argument during a basketball game the previous Easter weekend. As I walked off stage, I randomly spoke a word of encouragement to a young man seated in the front row. I don't know why I spoke to him of all people. It was beyond my understanding, but it would prove to be a significant moment brought on by God for both of us.

I couldn't stop thinking about the young man the rest of the night and the next day, so I told another counselor about the experience. He believed that God might have put the young man on my heart for me to talk with him and suggested I do so. As we were talking, the young man walked out of the building and right in front of the car where we were sitting!

The timing was extraordinary yet in line with all that had happened the night before. As my friend left, I called the young man over and asked if I could speak to him for a minute. To my surprise, he didn't look at all shocked to see me. He acted as if he already knew something was up. I invited him to sit with me in the car due to the rain coming down and I introduced myself. I explained I couldn't stop thinking about him since last night's testimony time and that I believed the Lord was placing him on my heart, prompting me to reach out.

The young man replied respectfully, yet with irritation in his voice, he spoke, "Man, can I ask you a question?"

"Yes," I replied.

"Did my counselors put you up to talk with me?"

"No," I assured him with a puzzled look on my face.

"Are you sure? Nobody said nothin' to you about me?"

I raised my hand in the air as though I were taking a sworn oath, while giving him my best expression of innocence. Why was he adamant that someone else made me talk to him?

"Man, nobody has told me anything about you. You have just been on my heart," I replied, attempting to assure him.

He appeared convinced I was telling the truth, and then he told me his story. "Well, before I came here, my brother got stabbed, and I was thinking about getting the guy back."

I was stunned about what I discerned as the supernatural intervention of God in this person's life. Not that it was surprising God could, but that He was involving me, and the way He was doing it. I assured the young man that our meeting wasn't a set-up or orchestrated by man, but by God. Little did I know that later that evening, I would witness another level of spiritual warfare and the Almighty power of God.

Saturday evening, the auditorium was filled with youth and their adult chaperones. The preacher speaking that evening was a man named Rev. Jones, and the message focused on the Bible story of the fiery furnace and the three Hebrew boys, Shadrach, Meshach, Abednego. His message was titled "Bow or Burn."

The powerful and convicting message only intensified the electrifying atmosphere. This was more than a typical mood of a great concert or presentation. This was heavy and supernatural. During the message, I witnessed young men who came to the retreat to meet girls break down emotionally from the presence of God in the room.

Near the end of the message, Rev. Jones did something that sparked praise for God I had never witnessed before. He was so filled with the power of the Holy Spirit that he spun around in praise near the end of the sermon.

I joined others in the room, jumping, shouting, and praising God. Girls cried as if they were mourning, and young men hung their heads in sorrow. Most of the youth did not understand why they were feeling such remorse for their sin and brokenness before our perfect, holy God.

Though I was caught up in the praise as well, I was not overcome like some of the youth. Suddenly, a lady asked me if I was a minister because they needed help with a youth. I replied, "No," but she took hold of me, anyway. She led me to a group of women surrounding a young girl. The girl was lying on her back, weeping, overcome by the presence of God. I laid hands on her and prayed, but again, there was a call for leaders to come to another section of the auditorium, where there appeared to be an emergency. I believed God wanted to use me as a helper while on the retreat, so I walked toward the area. As I got closer, I noticed many youths were being moved out of the building and away from the incident.

When I arrived, I saw something bizarre. Three or four people restrained an irate, aggressive young girl. Her speech caught me off guard, both by what she said and how she said it. Instead of praising God like the others, she was cursing, and her voice had somehow changed to sound very sinister, as if someone else was using her voice box to speak. I then noticed the movement of her eyes darted from one person to the next abnormally as she cursed and made threats, "Let her go!! If y'all don't stop, I will kill her!"

For the first several minutes, I just observed and analyzed whether this was real. I observed the faces of the adults nearby. Chaperones from various churches all appeared shaken. Many of them stood far off, wanting nothing to do with the scary spectacle before them, while others stood by, wanting to help, but not knowing what to do.

I had read about it in the Bible, heard testimonies, and even watched depictions of it in the movies, but I had never witnessed a demon possession. As I watched the situation unfold, I told myself that this cannot be real. My generation had no time for fake spiritual occurrences set up to appear supernatural. We wanted nothing to do with false healings and prophecies that only hurt people and labeled all Christians as naive phonies seeking thrills and seduction.

Suddenly, the demon looked sternly at the top youth leader of the retreat and hissed, "I know something about you!"

Whether or not the demon was lying, the leader was noticeably shaken. He walked away, and a chill went down my back as I sensed this was not an act or a game. A few minutes later, the rescue squad arrived, confirming this was not a setup. They tried to treat the young lady, but they soon realized they had no equipment to treat a demonic spirit and left.

The demon inside her continued to make threats, saying hurtful things to us and to the girl. It kept telling the girl her grandmother never loved her and that it would kill her if we didn't let her go. A group of us tried to ignore the demon's obscenities by gathering around to sing praises to God, and to pray for the young girl's deliverance.

As we sang a song that referenced the power of the blood of Jesus, the demon spoke one of the most blasphemous songs I ever heard and squashed the last bit of doubt I had about the ordeal.

In a twisted rendition of, "Oh, Come all Ye Faithful," the demon sang, "Oh, come let us adore him. Oh, come let us adore him. Oh, come let us adore him... Satan the king."

Fortunately, God used a strong Christian man to help in properly ministering to the girl. I suspected he was a pastor as I observed how boldly and fearlessly confronted the demon, and how it responded to him. The demon tried to ignore the man as much as he could, appearing to recognize it was not dealing with a spiritual punk.

I admired his knowledge and courage to approach the powers of darkness to see this young soul set free. At his instruction, we continued to pray and sing, believing God would deliver this precious girl. Eventually, and with joy in our hearts, we saw the girl lying peacefully in the arms of a woman I assumed was her mother. God had shown Himself faithful and mighty!

I left the retreat the next day as a different man. As I thought about what the Lord had allowed me to experience, I realized the same youth who had been so passionate and on fire for God would fizzle out when they returned home to lukewarm or dead churches. I thought about how many people, including Christians, didn't believe in the demonic, and how many churches were unprepared, untaught, or indifferent to the area of deliverance. I thought about how many were blind to the depth of evil around them and to how real the spirit world is.

God truly protects us from dangers seen and unseen. The fire inside me to save souls and to see people become free increased. What God had allowed me to experience was for my growth and to share with others. Of course, God knew I was content behind the scenes in the street and the marketplaces, but I now sensed Him calling me beyond my familiar area of influence. The interesting thing was that, though it was out of my comfort zone, I had a desire to go. The question confronting me was how to follow His call.

> **I THOUGHT ABOUT HOW MANY WERE BLIND TO THE DEPTH OF EVIL AROUND THEM AND TO HOW REAL THE SPIRIT WORLD IS.**

CHAPTER 25

THE CALL

When I returned to Lottsburg, I met with my pastor to share my experience and desire to preach. I did not know if that meant youth ministry or something else; I just knew the passion and sense of duty to preach had increased. He said he'd seen this conversation coming a long time ago, so he was prepared to give me a book to help me discern specifically what God had planned for me.

The book was about the forgotten biblical teaching of prayer and fasting, and the many benefits that prayerful fasting brings to those who apply it to their lives properly. I was illuminated by what I learned, so I studied related Scriptures, only to become convicted and disheartened as I realized the modern American church did not teach the importance and effectiveness of this misunderstood practice.

As I discerned God's direction for me, I took it seriously. I was cool with preaching and teaching without a microphone or standing behind a podium. I just needed to know that I was the one who was sent. Just because someone knows a few scriptures and teaches Sunday school class doesn't mean they are called to full-time ministry.

After confiding in my wife, I fasted for the first time in my life. I prayed and asked God to speak to me and show me specifically if He was calling me into the ministry. On the third day of my fast, I intended to hear my pastor preach as a visiting minister at a nearby church. I truly believed in supporting one's pastor, and I knew I needed to set an example if I was going to be a leader. Yet, uncharacteristically, as time drew near, I didn't want to go. I wanted to be around the Word of God, but not where my pastor was preaching.

Instead, I wanted to attend the church nearby, led by Pastor Kearse. I admired and appreciated Pastor Kearse from the very first time I heard him teach. We had met once before outside of church and from that brief fellowship, I was moved by his genuine honesty and desire to please God.

I felt a divine connection to him that was hard to explain. Although our ages and life experiences were more than a decade apart, he appeared to be someone I could relate to and learn from as a mentor. I wanted to attend his church, but it seemed the Lord wanted me at the church in Lottsburg, which made my waning interest going to this service with my home church more bizarre.

I figured that, as the visiting church, our congregation would have more members in attendance than the host church. The service would consist of songs, jokes, pleasantries, and a brief sermon, but no souls would be convicted or saved. I'd been to these services many times before, and my spirit was tired of the status quo. I didn't care about religious activities conducted with dead emotional ritualism that left little to no fruit except a sense of pious religiosity for the evening. After what I had experienced on the youth retreat, I could accept nothing less than revival.

I needed a specific word for my life and deliverance from the lust that still crept up into my thoughts and actions. I still caved in to the lure of porn now and then, and it drained my spiritual confidence for weeks afterward. Porn was the kryptonite to my boldness and willingness to witness, and to my ability to confront to the very real powers of darkness I knew were not to be played with.

PORN WAS THE KRYPTONITE TO MY BOLDNESS AND WILLINGNESS TO WITNESS, AND TO MY ABILITY TO CONFRONT TO THE VERY REAL POWERS OF DARKNESS I KNEW WERE NOT TO BE PLAYED WITH.

Finally, it was time to hear my pastor preach as the visiting minister at the night service. I was unfamiliar with where to go, so I planned to drive behind other members. As I followed them, the desire not to go became so strong that I couldn't take it anymore. I suddenly ducked into the parking lot of Pastor Kearse's church, hoping that none of the members from my current church saw me.

My draw to the church made little sense, and I felt ashamed for ducking from the members of my church. Even I knew my actions would be considered extreme and indefensible. To make matters worse, as I parked the car and walked toward the church, I saw a young lady I knew the enemy had been using to tempt me. Our paths met, so I had no choice but to walk in with her.

"This is not good," I said to myself, "Not only am I going to another church while my pastor is preaching nearby, but I am walking in with a very pretty, single, young lady." Oh, the thought of the rumors alone should have made me to turn around, but it didn't. The draw to that service was too strong.

As we went inside and sat down, I was surprised to learn they were having a youth revival! I sat in my seat chatting lightly with the young lady about my surprise that the service wasn't a Bible study, while internally asking God to reveal to me if He was calling me into the ministry. Somehow, I politely excused myself and found another seat so I could focus.

As the service began, I learned the preacher for the night was a white man seated behind the pulpit. This was unusual, because white preachers rarely came to a predominately black church, unless it was a funeral. To see a white preacher at a revival in our area was extraordinary. It just confirmed my conviction about the pastor of the church and his desire for authentic Christianity.

The visiting preacher stated the message would be centered on John 21:15-17. His announcement stopped me mentally in my tracks and caused me to feel uneasy. I meditated on the same scripture the night before when I sensed God was speaking to me through it. I had read the entire Bible several times, but it was like I had never seen it before, which seemed odd to me. Out of all the scriptures I read the night before, it seemed as if God emphasized this passage the most.

> *So when they had dined, Jesus saith to Simon Peter, "Simon, son of Jonas, lovest thou me more than these?" He saith unto him, "Yea, Lord; thou knowest that I love thee." He saith unto him, "Feed my lambs."*
>
> *He saith to him again the second time, "Simon, son of Jonas, lovest thou me?" He saith unto him, "Yea, Lord; thou knowest that I love thee." He saith unto him, "Feed my sheep."*
>
> *He saith unto him the third time, "Simon, son of Jonas, lovest thou me?" Peter was grieved because he said unto him the third time, "Lovest thou me?" And he said unto him, "Lord, thou knowest all things; thou knowest that I love thee." Jesus saith unto him, "Feed my sheep.*
> *"* - John 21:15-17, (KJV)

When I read John 21:15-17, I saw a man who had denied and betrayed Jesus, and now had the opportunity to move beyond his past to be used by God to minister to the young and the older. When I saw Peter in this passage, I saw myself.

Though I loved God, I felt so unworthy and unfit to even be considered as a minister because of the adultery I committed and the lust I still battled. Yet, I felt a constant, undeniable conviction to witness the Gospel to the lost, strengthen other believers through teaching, and to be a man of godly integrity. Not wanting to see more into this than maybe it was, I considered it a coincidence and focused on the rest of the message.

After the message, the preacher ministered to people in untraditional ways compared to most Baptist churches I attended. I was inspired as I watched him operate in and use other spiritual gifts. I prayed as he ministered, asking God to speak to me and show me clearly if he was calling me to the ministry. I believed God would see my sincerity and faith through my prayer and fasting, and He would answer me.

After ministering to a certain couple, the preacher announced the Lord showed him He was calling a young man in the congregation into the ministry. I sat in a daze questioning if I had heard him correctly. Then once again he stated the Lord was calling a young man into ministry. Inside I was tripping. This couldn't be happening. Even though I had been praying in faith and believing that God would answer my prayer, it was almost unbelievable that He would answer in this way.

I didn't want to be presumptuous, so I remained seated and looked around to see if the call pertained to another young man. I waited to see who would respond, but no one came forward. Still, the preacher waited patiently in front of the and stated again that the Lord wanted him to anoint a young man called into the ministry.

I was nervous and still questioning if it was me. I didn't want to miss out on this supernatural answer, if indeed this was the answer, but neither did I want to embrace a moment that belonged to another, causing me to embrace a lie.

The preacher then began asking as if he could see or perceive a name that began with the letter A, but he didn't know how to pronounce it.

"Is there an Andy or Andrew, or . . . You know who you are!" He abruptly and confidently stated.

Almost immediately, the pastor and several others let out a little praise as if finally, they knew who the calling was for. A lady who sat across from me said, "Antwaun, it's you!"

More nervous than ever, I stood in fear that God would be angry with me for doubting and believing his faithfulness to answer my prayer. I slowly stood and walked toward the front, not sure what would happen when I got to the altar. The preacher said I had the gift of teaching and that the pastor of the church was to be my mentor. I was freaking out inside. I knew this information had to be revealed by God because this man did not know me, my desire or ability to teach, or my inner desire to be under the pastor's leadership.

The congregation celebrating my affirmation by God had no idea of just how supernatural and confirming it was. No one knew I had been praying and fasting for a specific answer from God concerning ministry, nor about my spiritual intuition concerning Pastor Kearse. Last, no one knew that not only did the preacher preach from the same text that I had read the night before, but that the Spirit led me to be there in the first place.

Yet, while all of this would have been convincing enough for most, I still had doubts. Afterward, I asked Pastor Kearse if he had a conversation concerning me with the visiting preacher. Maybe he mentioned something that may have influenced this supposed revelation about a young man being called to ministry. Though my asking him might have seemed disrespectful, I needed to be sure that God had used these men as instruments without their own influence.

Pastor Kearse assured me he said nothing to the visiting preacher about me, but about a week later, I asked him for the preacher's phone number so I could talk to him personally. His response blessed my soul. He told me that before he left his home in Texas that day, God told him there would be a young man who was going to be called to the ministry.

I knew deep down that only God could arrange these events. My conversation with the preacher silenced all doubts and accusations from Satan that this was all coincidence. How helpful this confirmation was as unseen internal and external storms brewed not far on the horizon.

CHAPTER 26

THE MENTOR AND THE STORM

I remained at my home church for close to a year after my public affirmation. During that first year, I did not understand why God didn't release me sooner, knowing that Pastor Kearse and I were at two different churches. I eventually understood God wanted me to learn a few things that would be valuable in the future.

I became a licensed minister, preached my first sermon, and I was teaching the adult men's Sunday school class. The church was growing quickly, but I sensed in my spirit that it was time to leave and join the fellowship under Pastor Kearse.

He became a mentor in a way reminiscent of Coach Stevenson except on a spiritual level. Like Coach Stevenson in basketball, I admired Pastor Kearse's vast knowledge and insight of the Scriptures, as well as his personal supernatural experiences with God that could not be taught or duplicated by studying doctrine.

Pastor Kearse became my spiritual father. He was bold, yet humble, distant, yet very transparent and personal. The things I admired most were his courage to speak the truth even in the face of persecution and misinterpretation, along with his hunger to know and please God more. He was the only pastor I knew that spoke and stood firmly against Free Masonry because it did not mix with the Christian faith.

He and I took issues with church members who appeared more concerned and committed to social and civil rights organizations than to the church and the Great Commission of God. Yes, we understood the seriousness of confronting systematic racism in our country and the need for justice, but it had to be done God's way.

For Pastor Kearse and me, the great commission was the first priority of the church, so nothing should ever come before it. Mark 8:36 says, "For what shall it profit a man, if he shall gain the whole world, and lose his own soul?" (KJV)

This position, along with other unpopular stances, brought expected but unjustified persecution against him, but through it all he stood firm in his desire to please God more than man. Still, Pastor Kearse felt he wasn't bold enough. He wanted to be stronger in doing what he believed the Lord instructed him to say or do.

I was encouraged, but truly challenged, to strive for excellence in all areas of my Christian walk. It was because of him I went back to college to earn an associate degree in Biblical Studies instead of wasting my time trying to relive or create vain hoop dreams in open gym. He tested my commitment several times, but the experience always strengthened and elevated us to a profound spiritual level.

I had the pleasure of working with Pastor Kearse's son in ministry, Mike. All three of us experienced and witnessed the supernatural power of God, but we wanted more. Pastor told Mike and I to meet at the church early two to three days per week to pray. I was not thrilled about getting up so early in the morning, but I understood it was necessary. As much as I loved my sleep, prayer is the price to seek the power of God and to see Him move as He has in the past.

Shortly after our prayer meetings began, we saw God move. We felt His influence as He convicted our hearts of how far the church had fallen away from what it was meant to be, and how many Christians were content with going to church and leaving their faith inside as they walked out.

HOW MANY CHRISTIANS ARE CONTENT WITH GOING TO CHURCH AND LEAVING THEIR FAITH INSIDE AS THEY WALK OUT.

I felt overwhelmed and frightened as God continued to enlighten my mind and tug at my heart. Again, like another matrix experience, God opened our eyes to see how evil and corrupt our world and country really are. The teachings and beliefs in a lot of America's churches are lukewarm and degenerate.

God's people are practicing logical insanity, thinking we can embrace the world and its sinful ways and still be cool with

God. Christians are misguided in the assumption that Satan worship is exclusive to practicing Satanists. Anyone who gives allegiance to anything before their allegiance to God has become an idol-worshipper.

HERE NOW WAS THE CHURCH, GOD'S PEOPLE PRACTICING LOGICAL INSANITY.

We sin every time we put more value and priority on gifted athletes, actors, singers, media hosts and other entertainers, than the God who made us. We make idols of the Constitution over the Bible and our temporary American residency over our identity as an eternal citizen in the kingdom of heaven.

Christians no longer understand the difference between what is holy and what is profane, as evidenced by debating issues that clearly shouldn't even be questioned. Should Christians celebrate Halloween, a day dedicated to evil? Should we accept that young black men die in the streets and go to prison by the thousands, and neither white nor black Christians appear righteously indignant about it?

We have become professing Christians but practicing atheists. I prayed fervently for wisdom and guidance. "Lord, how do we express these profanities to people who seek a convenient, yet compromised gospel from preachers and teachers too afraid to preach biblical truth? How do we declare Your truth to people who don't read Your Word, so they can't recognize false prophets?

People embrace lies because they fear persecution. How do we strengthen them to live in Your truth despite fears of losing friends, jobs, positions, and even their life for Your name if need be?"

WE HAVE BECOME PROFESSING CHRISTIANS, BUT PRACTICING ATHEISTS.

God stirred a zeal and passion in my heart that scared me as I considered the burden of this knowledge and the cost of speaking out. I wondered if this was how Jeremiah, Elijah, Paul, Martin Luther, and Martin Luther King Jr. felt as they were compelled to stand for truth. They must have known their name could be cast out with contempt, that they would be called narrow-minded, judgmental, hateful, negative, fanatics, and bigots by people who confused righteous anger toward sin with hatred toward man. I sensed these men suspected they could lose their lives to people who claimed to be doing the will of God.

The fire brewing in all three of us could not be contained. We were bound to meet the coldness in the hearts of many. In fact, strife quickly manifested in overt and disrespectful ways.

Confrontation was inevitable, and just like when a cold front slams against the heat of a sweltering day, there was about to be a storm.

CHAPTER 27

THE STORM

I patiently anticipated Pastor Kearse's message as the service began. A few days prior, he asked me to pray for him as he prepared a challenging and potentially controversial sermon. This was a rare request, and although I did not know the topic, I knew he was not only prepared to preach it, but that he could handle any backlash or persecution.

Our prayer time preceding this day brought about a boldness tempered by our awareness of our own need to fully surrender certain areas of our lives. I had previously stepped down from ministering twice, first by my own volition following a conversation with Pastor, and the second following leaders' false allegations regarding my unbecoming behavior in the community. The alleged behavior involved a fight that never occurred, but I submitted without defense because I had been part of stupid arguments while playing ball in the gym. The disagreements did not escalate to a fight, but my behavior still did not meet the standard of a minister or leader found in the First Book of Timothy.

I knew getting myself together was more important than exposing the motives of those who sought to embarrass and discredit me. Despite the embarrassment, I was relieved for the opportunity to humble myself before God. Being right with God far exceeds worrying about those who might rejoice in my pain, for I believe the Scripture in 1 Corinthians 11:30–32 that says, "For if we would judge ourselves, we should not be judged." (KJV)

I listened to Pastor Kearse testify to how the Lord showed him he needed to repent. Unknown to him, his wife Lynn had asked the Lord to speak, even if He had to speak through their two-year old son. While Pastor and his wife were praying, God miraculously opened the mouth of his toddler, and he said, "Repent."

Pastor testified that not long after, the Spirit of God expressed no one, including him, was above the standard clearly revealed in His Word. God said Pastor needed to repent and the retraining of some current leaders would have to occur. He listed reasonable, yet imperative qualities that should be the norm for all Christians witnessing, teaching, or attending Bible study. These qualities were especially critical for leaders who understand their commission and purpose given by God.

This was not the entire message, but it was the part that angered a few influential church leaders with a very different vision and agenda. Shortly after this memorable service, a few select leaders held a secret meeting to oust Pastor Kearse from the church. Unknown to me and many others, they formed a conspiracy and gave their unanimous vote to attain worldly legal authority to remove him.

Soon after, Pastor received a legal notice informing him not to enter the church. He disobeyed, knowing the decree was improper, unjust, and issued deceitfully without the knowledge of most church members. A day or two later, Carolyn called me at work to notify me that Pastor was in jail. I calmly told her he was going to be ok. Our weeks of praying and seeking God's face along with Pastor's own private devotion had prepared him for this moment.

A few days later, I found out about another secret meeting, and I went to speak out against the conspiracy. As I rebuked the conspirators, one of them quickly left to call the police. Another member in attendance convinced the leader to put his phone away, but the response told me where their hearts were. They had no interest in discussion, or prayer, or searching God's Word. They just wanted me and Pastor Kearse to leave.

I spoke out against the ungodly nature of the conspirators' actions again during Sunday school the following week, so I was not surprised to find a notice from the sheriff's office on my car window after service. I drove to the sheriff's office and met the officer who issued the notice. He appeared bothered by what he'd been forced to do. He apologized and informed me I was no longer to go on church grounds.

I smiled and rejoiced inside as though the notice was an honorary degree. I understood I was being persecuted not for doing evil, but for doing good. The Word says to, "rejoice and be exceedingly glad" when persecuted, so that was exactly what I was aiming to do. (Matthew 5:12 KJV)

As for Pastor, he waited patiently and sought God on what to do. Many from the church who loved Pastor and were blessed by his ministry felt confused, hurt, and angry. His sudden departure caught them off guard, struggling to understand how such a crazy thing could happen so fast and without the congregation's knowledge. Many members vowed to leave with Pastor. Rather than support any kind of division, Pastor Kearse continued to listen for God and to be led by the Spirit. Instead of challenging the rebellion, he let go peacefully, and a new ministry was born.

The new ministry grew quickly and steadily through a fresh spirit of hope and sincere love. I watched as hurting people found love and healing inside our fellowship. I saw men saved, and strongholds of addiction and fragmented families come together. One young girl who visited found wise council and comfort from being tormented by supernatural things she didn't understand.

What a time it was to see the power of God move after all that we had been through. What a blessing it was to be part of a church where the saving of souls was seen not as a suggestion but as a command.

Yet, we still endured attacks from without and within. I learned that reformation comes with a cost. To trust God completely, a man must be truly dead to self, always putting things of God before his own desires, for it shakes the demons of hell to see a holy vision come to life and bring glory to God. Increasingly, I was understanding more the truth of a statement that I had once heard from a great man of God: "The purer the intent, the greater the opposition."

I LEARNED THAT REFORMATION COMES WITH A COST. TO TRUST GOD COMPLETELY, A MAN MUST BE TRULY DEAD TO SELF, ALWAYS PUTTING THINGS OF GOD BEFORE HIS OWN DESIRES, FOR IT SHAKES THE DEMONS OF HELL TO SEE A HOLY VISION COME TO LIFE AND BRING GLORY TO GOD.

CHAPTER 28

SLIP, SLIDING AWAY

Before the church storm occurred, I met a young man named Neal at the school gym. Although I knew him for a brief time, he left a lasting impression on my life. I heard about Neal from others in the community shortly before he got out of jail. He had a reputation for being "about that life," and he was not afraid of violence.

I took notice of how people greeted and responded to Neal when he came to play basketball during open gym. I could tell he had much respect. I observed his interactions discreetly while hoping I wouldn't have to speak to him about bringing drama inside. At some point, we politely spoke to each other. Our greeting was brief, and nothing suggested the slightest interest of either of us to know the other, which made our encounter later extremely special.

One evening I stopped at the Food Lion after basketball. On my way out of the store, I spotted Neal and his cousin sitting in a car. Both were just chilling, as though they were waiting to meet someone. Suddenly, I sensed God wanted me to witness to him. I thought there could have been a better place and time, but I also knew God didn't wait for the most convenient moment to nudge His messenger to deliver a message. Even though I didn't have any rapport with Neal, I knew it was better to obey than risk hearing something happened to him the next day and I missed fulfilling an important assignment.

> *SUDDENLY, I SENSED GOD WANTED ME TO WITNESS TO HIM. I THOUGHT THERE COULD HAVE BEEN A BETTER PLACE AND TIME, BUT I ALSO KNEW GOD DIDN'T WAIT FOR THE MOST CONVENIENT MOMENT TO NUDGE HIS MESSENGER TO DELIVER A MESSAGE.*

I walked up to the car and began talking to them. Although he kept his cool demeanor, I was surprised to see that Neal appeared to be receptive to my message. I can't remember all that I shared with them, but I do recall warning them about potential jail time and how death could come from living the fast life. More importantly, I let them know that choosing Jesus was the best decision they could ever make in their lives. His cousin seemed annoyed with me, and though Neal seemed appreciative, I wasn't sure how seriously he took my words.

Unfortunately, I found out soon after that he was arrested again and received approximately a two-year sentence. I wondered if he spent any of his time in lock-up considering our brief encounter and my warning. I would find out when God reconnected us in the most peculiar way.

CHAPTER 29

JUST LIKE FAMILY

Almost three years after Neal went to jail, I served as an assistant coach for the girls' JV basketball team in Northumberland. Tryouts for the team were almost finished. I just had to make the final cuts before announcing the team roster for the year.

Sometimes I wondered if cutting players was harder on me than it was for the kids. At the start of tryouts, there was one young lady whose lack of basketball experience and skill showed no reason to keep her on the team. Yet, Moniqua not only improved a little each day, but she had a bigger heart than any other player out there. She wanted it and she was physical! Having the heart for the game was not enough reason to keep her, but her determination, strong desire to learn, and untapped physical potential were hard to ignore. For these reasons, I couldn't deny her or the team from having her on board.

Over time, Moniqua became like a little sister to me. She even attended church with my family. One day, when I took her home from practice, I noticed a muscular young man waving and smiling as though he knew me. "Who is that?" I asked Moniqua.

"Oh, that's my uncle Neal," she replied.

I looked again and sure enough, it was the same Neal I had witnessed to several years before, just noticeably bigger since his time in jail. I stepped out of the car and met him and shared a quick brotherly embrace as though we had been boys for years. As we chatted, I asked him if he remembered what I had told him about the night at the Food Lion prior to his getting locked up.

He said he did, so I reminded him the warning still applied, and that the devil was still waiting to destroy God's purpose for his life. I reminded him that the same friends and acquaintances from the past were going to want to "kick it" again, which could lead him back to the negative lifestyle.

He agreed, but we both knew it was easier said than done. I invited him to church and offered to give him a ride to service. He immediately agreed to go with me, but his verbal commitment was much quicker than his follow through. Every Sunday for weeks brought a similar excuse. The delay was not a surprise, but I had to follow through so he would know I was serious about supporting him. I just perceived that the streets would be calling Neal with drama that might have him back in jail, or worse.

Sure enough, drama came. One evening while taking Moniqua home from practice, she asked me if it was ok for Christians to go to night clubs. "No," I replied while explaining the propensity clubs had for sin, especially worldly lust and violence. "It's the devil's playground," I concluded, "where anyone can be affected in a bad way."

Moniqua was silent for a moment but then stated, "Coach, this may sound bad, but I almost wish that I had not gotten saved, 'cause I have never been to a club before, and I really want to see what one is like."

I understood the frustration of fighting the strong curiosity of experiencing something just once, even though you know God would disapprove. Her internal conflict to honor her commitment to God despite the temptation and risk is a dilemma many Christians wrestle with. It is especially confusing for kids when the world, and even some in the church, allows or participates in certain activities that conflict with the Word of God.

At that moment, I brought her attention to the beauty and magnificence of the orange sun setting in the distance as a demonstration of how awesome the God who created it had to be. Then, I repeated something I had heard in a sermon. "Moniqua, always remember, you can choose the sin, but you cannot choose the consequence." I dropped her off, hoping she would meditate and be convicted by what I said. I had no idea of how quickly the revelation would come to her.

Within a few hours, Moniqua called me crying. Neal was stabbed in the stomach while at the club. He was cut badly, but it wasn't life threatening. I then asked her softly if she understood now what I tried to tell her earlier in the car, to which she humbly said, "Yes." Though I didn't take pleasure in seeing Neal hurt, I was comforted by the timing of his trouble—trouble God used to speak to his niece.

The next day, I went to the hospital to visit Neal. He had a tube in his nose and was in pain. He gave me a warm smile that exposed his gold tooth. After I asked how he was doing, I abruptly shifted the conversation. I asked him if he understood the seriousness of the devil's intent to destroy him. He said "Yes," and prayed with me to receive Jesus as his Lord and Savior.

Our church was still wholly under Pastor Kearse's leadership at the time Neal got out of the hospital and joined me for service. I rejoiced the day he was baptized. It was a joy to see him in church, especially when he brought family members with him. He shared testimonies of how friends and family noticed he seemed different. Even the sound of his voice over the phone had changed. He told me one of his former running partners could not believe it when Neal asked him to take him to church instead of some hot spot or a woman's house. His smile as he shared events like this showed the newfound happiness and joy he had from finding strength within to win one battle at a time.

I loved him like a little brother, so I called him "Bro." Neal was such a blessing that I encouraged Antwaun Jr. to call him "uncle," a title I never imagined for him a few years prior. In my eyes, Neal was family. He was my brother in Christ, and I truly wanted to guide my new bro to the best of my ability. But just as if planned by some evil force, an abrupt interruption occurred in both our lives.

When the confusion of the storm occurred at church, some members became disgruntled with the madness. Pastor was banned from the church, so while the human shepherd was smitten by false accusations that kept him from his flock, Neal was one of the sheep that scattered. Then, I was banned from the church and with home responsibilities and up to fourteen-hour workdays, I lost weekly contact with Neal.

One night, I attended a high school basketball game with my friend Mike. We saw Neal at a distance and waved. He waved back and smiled somewhat, but he continued going the other way. I intuitively knew something was wrong. Both Mike and I picked up on the change. We had seen it before. Normally, Neal headed in my direction to embrace and chat, but his demeanor was as if he didn't want me to know that something was wrong. I suspected he had backslidden in his walk with God.

I figured we would get together, talk about the church drama, fellowshipping at a new place, and his spiritual wellbeing, but that time never came. Not long after, I received a call from Pastor to tell me Neal was shot at the lodge. I felt uneasy when Pastor asked if I wanted him to come get me, so I met at his house instead. As I raced to Pastor's house, I remembered our first conversation at the Food Lion, along with other warnings I had shared with Neal over the years. I prayed for his life as I tried to fight off negative thoughts.

I got to Pastor's house in no time, jumped in his van, and proceeded to the hospital. Pastor prayed, and I joined quietly with him in unison. Then suddenly I heard him say something like, "Lord, we ask that Neals' death won't be in vain, but that people would be convicted and give their lives to You."

Inside, I felt disconnected and caught off guard by Pastor's seemingly presumptuous prayer. I was bothered, but I waited until he finished praying. As soon as he was done, I immediately asked him why he had spoken of Neal as being dead instead of praying to keep him from death. What he told me troubled my soul and brought sorrow that would only increase later.

He informed me that recently, while he was heading home, that God spoke to him, telling him to turn his vehicle around and give a warning to Neal. The warning was that if he didn't stop doing what he was involved in, he was going to die. He confidently told me that Neal would be dead before we got to the hospital. I then understood that Pastor's confidence in what God told him concerning Neal was why he expected to see the result of what God had said would happen to him. Pastor loved Neal and wanted him alive, but he understood the seriousness of the warning. When we arrived at the hospital, I quickly noticed the crowd outside. Their tears were not from concern; they were mourning.

I got out of the van and ran inside the hospital, where I met up with Mike. We both went inside to see Neal for ourselves. We walked toward the room and around a partially opened curtain to find Neal lying lifeless on the table. The suffering reflected on his face caused my heart to bypass my grief. Instead, I felt an abrupt surge of anger as I looked at a young man with great potential, but was now a casualty of the spiritual war many people didn't know existed.

I FELT AN ABRUPT SURGE OF ANGER AS I LOOKED AT A YOUNG MAN WITH GREAT POTENTIAL WHO WAS NOW A CASUALTY OF THE SPIRITUAL WAR MANY PEOPLE DIDN'T KNOW EXISTED.

This was not supposed to be his ending. Not like this. I thought about how it was only by the grace and mercy of God that it wasn't me lying there. I wondered how to tell Antwaun Jr. that he wouldn't see Uncle Neal anymore. I thought about how I would never see Neal's simple smile exposing the gold tooth.

An inescapable principle of both the saved and the unsaved caught up with Neal early in his life: "The wages of sin is death." (Romans 6:23 KJV)

As I went home that day, the only solace I could find was that, even though he had backslidden in his new walk with the Lord, Neal was saved.

Information I learned about the circumstances of the shooting seemed to support my beliefs about his genuine change. Neal was shot trying to break up a fight, possibly taking a bullet meant for someone else. If that was the case, then he had left this world trying to be a peacemaker and unknowingly laid down his life for another.

From the day of his funeral, where a number of souls came forward to give their life to Christ, till now, I have endeavored to make sure his name and story would not be forgotten. My hope is that by sharing his story, those who see themselves in Neal would heed the warnings already spoken in their ears and hearts by loving messengers sent from God. And maybe—just maybe—another soldier won't be an unnecessary casualty of spiritual war.

CHAPTER 30

PRODIGAL SON

Neal was gone, the ministry seemed to be constantly under attack from both the outside and from within, and I struggled in my Christian walk like never before. Compromised thoughts led to a compromised walk when the purchase of a computer to take online classes opened an old destructive door of temptation.

COMPROMISED THOUGHTS LED TO A COMPROMISED WALK.

This time, access to the porn was much easier and cheaper. The information superhighway offered an endless journey to a world where any traveler could view thousands of beautiful, physically sculptured women posing and involved in the most seductive and explicit acts. Their eyes gazed through the monitor saying, "I want you," as if I was the only one she desired, when in reality, she spoke to millions of other men and women the same way.

Suddenly, I saw them for who they really were—lost, abandoned, neglected, or abused daughters—not as sexual objects, but as someone's mother, aunt, niece, daughter, or sister.

When I found chat rooms, a perplexing and even more dangerous cycle of behavior emerged. The women in chat rooms, whether religious or non-religious, were not as overt with their sinful desires. They were also looking for solace in artificial love.

I fell deeper into infidelity through sexual conversations and virtual affairs with women in the US and overseas. The women I met in chat rooms knew me as a schizophrenic-like man. First, I appealed to their hidden desires through romantic and sensual conversations so many of the women wanted to meet me. Then the next powerful sermon I heard strengthened me to minister to them and end the affair. I brought them to tears through strong conviction of their behavior from the Word of God, followed by an assurance that they needed God instead of me, real love rather than lust.

But no woman hurt more from my dichotomy of switching from spirit to flesh than Carolyn. She'd see me meditating in the Word and in tearful prayers for others in the middle of the night, only to be neglected for women I never met the next night.

I tried to hide my virtual affairs from Carolyn, but she caught on to the lies and endured the painful rejection in silence. I could see the agony on her face when I refused to come to bed with her with some lame excuse. If she asked me what I was doing on the computer, I responded defensively, she would apologize for her accusations, and I continued my behavior.

My conduct was not only unbecoming at home and in the community, but arguments at the gym became more frequent and intense as my actions failed to resemble the behavior of a true minister, or even a Christian, for that matter. My heart screamed "hypocrite" louder and louder, but I showed signs of breaking from the guilt and condemnation.

> **MY CONDUCT WAS NOT ONLY UNBECOMING AT HOME AND IN THE COMMUNITY, BUT ARGUMENTS AT THE GYM BECAME MORE FREQUENT AND INTENSE AS MY ACTIONS FAILED TO RESEMBLE THE BEHAVIOR OF A TRUE MINISTER, OR EVEN A CHRISTIAN FOR THAT MATTER. MY HEART SCREAMED "HYPOCRITE" LOUDER AND LOUDER, BUT I SHOWED SIGNS OF BREAKING FROM THE GUILT AND CONDEMNATION.**

Overcome by grief and exhaustion, I broke down and screamed words I had never spoken before, "Daddy, I need You! Daddy, I need You!" I felt like a little child who wanted to be held by his father like the time Father held me that special day in Washington DC many years ago. I wanted to ask him if he struggled like this, and though I didn't say his name, I thought of Marvin as well.

Father had died a couple of years before. I found out through my aunt while I was driving. She told me his death was announced in Jet Magazine, so I pulled into the next gas station to buy the magazine. Guilt and loneliness came upon me as I stood inside the gas station reading the article. The loneliness came from the sense of abandonment and the realization that there would never be another earthly reunion as I had hoped. At the same time, I felt I may have abandoned him. I wondered if Father died alone, hoping his young son in Virginia would come to his side.

Carolyn was concerned as she watched all these thoughts and feelings unfold. I normally like referring to myself and other Christians as soldiers, but I was depleted of strength and weary of fighting the lust and pride within myself. I resisted God in my refusal to "let us lay aside every weight, and the sin which doth so easily beset us." (Hebrews 12:1 KJV) Even weights that were not sinful in themselves, such as basketball, had become idols and distractions hindering the call of God on my life. Basically, I was bucking and saying, "Not His will but mine be done."

In my quiet time with God, He highlighted the scripture that said "Ye are not your own, for ye are bought with a price."
(1 Corinthians 6:19 KJV) I realized that I truly didn't understand I had given up my rights to be my own god, my own lord and master. I had to relinquish not only my talent and gifts but also my time. It was only when God asked me to give up the time I spent in certain activities that I saw how much of an idol they were to me. By refusing to surrender weights, it was easier to yield and be overcome to lust and vain glory. I was learning the hard way that selfishness would not take me to my desired destination, but only cause me to backslide on a road called "slip-sliding away".

CHAPTER 31

RUNNING AWAY

I noticed the woman when she came in the church. Immediately, my heart raced with an intense desire to hide. Though she was not a member or regular attendee, I had had some prior dealings with her that I sensed could lead to a possible physical encounter.

We occasionally bumped into each other in public and had brief conversations about work, sports, and church. Inviting her to church was how I tried to get in my own way in battling lustful thoughts. The only problem was there appeared to be an unspoken mutual attraction, an almost palpable lust. So here I was, sitting in church, uneasy during the entire service and struggling to focus on the Word because of her presence.

When Pastor finished his sermon, he invited anyone who wanted to pray or surrender to God to come to the front of church. As was the normal routine, Pastor and I stood in the front of the aisle waiting for anyone who came forward. I noticed the woman got up from her seat and came forward for prayer. I dreaded the possibility of praying with her.

Fortunately, someone else prayed for her, but the crazy predicament was too much. If there was one place where my reverence for God brought about a fear and dread to sin against Him, it was in a place of worship. This was one place where I felt safe from the attacks of lustful thoughts, but that somehow seemed to fade. Something had to give. I couldn't continue like this. The last thing I needed was for an attractive woman battling with lust within her to come to church and not only detect it in me, but entertain it in subtle ways.

I sensed Pastor knew something wasn't right because of my lack of enthusiasm during worship and my absence at Bible study. I was supposed to be his armor bearer, his right-hand man, but I was becoming an undependable no-show. According to the scriptures, "Confidence in an unfaithful man in time of trouble is like a broken tooth and a foot out of joint." (Proverbs 25:19 KJV) A useless burden is what I had become to Pastor, and I would soon see my mentor leave.

Again, my pride and shame wouldn't let me tell anyone how bad it was. I hated the fact that my behavior matched some of the false rumors about me in the past. Even though I wasn't physically in bed with anyone, my heart was. I still thought I could find a breakthrough and shake off the madness without help. Such a foolish notion only led to more bondage and unfortunately, more mental and emotional suffering for Carolyn.

The condemnation and guilt were so unbearable that I stopped going to church. I just couldn't pretend everything was okay anymore. I was tired of the inconsistency in my life. One week, I was walking above lust and praising God for victory, only to return to it and become even more consumed than before. If "a double-minded man is unstable in all of his ways," (James 1:8 KJV) then I was disqualified from being an effective leader at church and at home.

ONE WEEK, I WAS WALKING ABOVE LUST AND PRAISING GOD FOR VICTORY, ONLY TO RETURN TO IT AND BECOME EVEN MORE CONSUMED THAN BEFORE.

Just as I couldn't bear to see the look of frustration in my Pastor's eyes anymore, I couldn't take the stress, damage, and suffering I caused the most precious woman in my life. Carolyn's tears increased each night she awoke and found me sitting at the computer instead of lying beside her. She knew she was getting my physical and emotional leftovers after my virtual adulterous escapades.

As I ran from ministry, I also ran from my marriage. Carolyn didn't deserve this. She wondered if my wandering was her fault. Her idea that she wasn't pretty or sensual enough was crazy to me, and even though I tried to reassure her, my actions reinforced her growing insecurities. In the past, I would wonder how anyone could walk out on their family without explanation and never return. I am in no way justifying it, but I understand now. At this time in my life, I just wanted to escape it all.

The strong sense of failure coupled with the ache of wounding and abusing my darling wife made me want to remove myself from the whole equation. Ruining my life was one thing, but ruining hers was another. I was too selfish and weak to give up the addiction, so leaving seemed to be the only logical solution. Surely a godly man with less baggage would find this beautiful and virtuous woman. Someone would love her and support her as she desired and deserved. These lies from the enemy pierced my mind and covered my soul over and over again.

The day I was slow to answer her question if I was still in love with her, followed by the suggestion that maybe we weren't meant to be together, was the day that I watched the woman I love die in front of me even though she was still breathing. I felt assured she was leaving, and I assumed the death of our marriage was inevitable.

Soon after that conversation, I found her lying on the bed with a glazed look on her face and an empty bottle of pills beside her. I realized how precious her heart was, and the possibility of losing her this way terrified me beyond measure. Our sweet children walked in just as I held their mother crying out, "Why!" "Why!" "Why!"

How was I a minister who didn't have the natural or spiritual sensitivity to detect a problem before tragedy occurred in my own marriage? How would I explain and be truthful about why my wife, my best friend, would try to overdose?

No woman or man is worth a person attempting to take their own life, but I learned that in Carolyn's mind, I was her life, the very air she breathed.

I never wanted or desired that kind of influence over another human being, but I understood that until Carolyn could see that she gave me the place in her heart that only God should have, I would not leave her. To be indirectly responsible for her death in that way, and to see our children grow up without their mother would have killed me with despair and guilt. She survived, and, my plan of running away to Stafford solo to start afresh changed. We were all going. If "He that troubleth his own house shall inherit the wind," Proverbs 11:29 (KJV) then my future actions would testify that the wind was just beginning to blow.

CHAPTER 32

FALLING DEEPER

Here I was on a Friday night, watching a woman walk inside the building as the faint sound of a bass and familiar musical rhythm pierced through the walls. I sat in the car with the windows down wondering how I had come to the point in my life of not just sitting outside of a club, but considering going in.

The last time I was outside of a club was in Lancaster, Virginia, I passed out Bible tracks as though I was distributing voter information during an important election. I also tried to catch and send home underage students trying to sneak in. I preached against clubs to youth and young adults for thirteen years, now here I was, going back in.

I was so uncomfortable my first time back at a club. I tried to ignore thoughts of Lot's wife in the Bible, thinking that something terrible would happen for turning back to a place that I didn't belong, and I was paranoid someone would recognize me even though I was far from anywhere I ever called home.

Unlike the verse in the theme song from the TV show Cheers, I wanted to be somewhere where nobody knew my name, somewhere I would blend in and get lost in the crowd. I was stuck in this rebellious state, but I didn't want anyone that I knew to witness it, be taken down by it, or to see how far I had fallen. I was there to entertain my lust as discreetly as possible. Though I loved to dance and to use my talent, it grieved me inside to hear lyrics contrary to God's Word and dance to music I despised. But I allowed my lust to override the Spirit's conviction. The attention from women reawakened the old feelings of vanity and the need to be liked and desired.

Using the influence of worldly charm and skillful dancing made it hard to go un-noticed. But as I danced, a great conflict took place. No one knew how severely distressed and depressed I was. I cringed when other men complemented on the appeal and number of women dancing with me. I felt terrible every time a lady thought she had found her soulmate in me. No matter how good of a catch or prospect I appeared to be, the truth was I was married, off limits, struggling with lust, and filled with selfishness.

Even if a woman were to convince me to leave Carolyn, my struggle would only hurt them like it was hurting her. I continued to crush her with lies to explain why I came home late or not at all. I protected my cell phone like it was issued by the CIA and that it was only to be answered by me, lest someone in the house should violate a federal law. Sometimes I forgot to hide my phone while I slept, which gave Carolyn the opportunity to confirm her suspicions.

When confronted, I would either avoid talking about it or downplay it as only inappropriate conversations and nothing more. I knew my behavior tortured Carolyn. After her first nervous breakdown, I lied as convincingly as I could for fear she would harm herself again, even as every word reminded me I was living a lie and out of the will of God.

Sometimes I confessed and pledged my desire to truly break free from the lying and adultery, but I would always go back. This back and forth believing that I would not return to bondage caused me to become even more discouraged and drained my will to fight.

The cycle of madness continued to take a toll on Carolyn. Sometimes, I would find her lying in bed incoherent, as if she were drugged. Her repeated breakdowns eventually left her too overwhelmed to work, which forced me to work other jobs to make up for the missed income. She also had violent outbursts. She hit things wildly, with no regard to her personal welfare. Sometimes I had to restrain her to keep her from hurting herself or beg her to calm down so the children wouldn't hear the commotion.

One day, I was too slow in grabbing her before she hit a glass candle holder. Broken glass pierced into her wrist as she threw her arm into it. She looked at me with shock and agony at the sight of blood flowing around the glass protruding from her arm. Just like when Carolyn overdosed, I became overcome and cried, "Why!" "Why!" "Why!" just as our children ran in the room to see the anxiety and fear on the faces of their parents.

Neither Antwaun Jr. nor Chante' knew their daddy created the storm they were suddenly privy to. And they didn't understand that their mother's unhealthy tolerance for Daddy's mess and her fear of losing him was slowly killing her.

"Why did Mother do that?" I remember my son saying as he tried to understand the confusion. "Mother, why did you hurt yourself?" he asked in anger toward her for causing him and his daddy stress.

The consequences of my sin were utterly destroying my family. I could not contain the repercussions to just me, no matter how hard I tried. Trying to manipulate how things would go was not working. I hated myself, for I knew the only one to blame was me. As I had told Moniqua in my car years before, I was learning more than ever that "You can choose the sin but you cannot choose the consequences."

"YOU CAN CHOOSE THE SIN, BUT YOU CANNOT CHOOSE THE CONSEQUENCES."

CHAPTER 33

STUPID MINDED

Had I fooled myself all these years living in deception thinking that I loved God, but I really loved only myself? Where did I go? Who is the real me? How did I ever come to this place?

A man who once hungered and thirsted for God's Word was now yielding to a forbidden, insatiable desire. Whispers of death constantly warned me the end was not far away. I was afraid to close my eyes at night, fearing that I would open my eyes in hell with no way out and no reprieve.

My car became a moving confessional, a mobile sanctuary, where I wailed and, pleaded with God to break my will and to save me from myself. I also wanted to know more about my brother Marvin through his music. As I heard his voice, I felt his love and pain. I sang with him, certain he fought similar battles in his own heart. The more I listened to my big brother, the more I believed I was traveling on the same road he had been on, and if I didn't get off soon, the journey would destroy me, too.

I chose to believe the love I heard flowing through him would embraced me, telling me he understood my pain and the cravings I hated. I knew very little about my brother Frankie other than that he had died several years prior. Since Frankie, Marvin Jr., and I were cut from the same DNA, I figured they would relate to me like no other man could. Since I couldn't speak with either of them, I continued singing with Marvin in the car.

I believed that the same evil spirits that had oppressed and sought to destroy them were now determined to destroy me using the weapons of the world: "the lust of the eyes and the flesh and the pride of life" (1 John 2:16 KJV). Together they form a wicked elixir meant to intoxicate, obscure, and distort one's view of true reality. These weapons keep us focused on pleasure while blinding us from impending doom.

THE SAME EVIL SPIRITS THAT HAD OPPRESSED AND SOUGHT TO DESTROY THEM WERE NOW DETERMINED TO DESTROY ME USING THE WEAPONS OF THE WORLD: THE LUST OF THE EYES AND THE FLESH AND THE PRIDE OF LIFE. TOGETHER THEY FORM A WICKED ELIXIR MEANT TO INTOXICATE, OBSCURE, AND DISTORT ONE'S VIEW OF TRUE REALITY.

As my behavior continued, I offered up my precious family in exchange for self-gratification. My children began displaying rebellious behavior at home and school because I was either too preoccupied with work or engaged in my selfish hobbies rather than spending quality time with them. Carolyn confessed she struggled to shake off flatteries from other men, even though she knew they had ulterior motives. The shame and guilt of my own choices caused me to condemn and isolate myself from the body of Christ. All these things pushed me to escape from reality and into the night.

I even doubted my salvation. Sometimes I felt like the man in the Bible who was delivered from affliction only to have the evil spirit come back with seven more spirits more wicked than the first (Matthew 12:43-45 KJV). Was that what was happening?

The stress of my sins showed up in my health when I had my first panic attack during a workout at the gym. My selfishness and self-hatred could no longer be contained. My soul had been immersed in madness for too long.

Emotionally I was spent. I was spent from feeling responsible to women who developed feelings for me. Spent from trying to keep my family problems a secret. Spent from getting two women pregnant only to lose both children. One child was lost to an unwanted abortion, and the other child because of complications during the mother's pregnancy. Carolyn knew about both pregnancies, and she was still willing to accept them. I was exhausted from seeing my son become more defiant until I had to visit him in the same detention center where I had worked. I was broken from seeing my daughter so stressed that I had to visit her in a hospital. I was worn down from seeing Mother physically removed from the house by sheriffs and sent back to the mental facility. My anxiety attacks increased, and I lost sleep and weight.

Carolyn's physical and emotional depletion was even more severe. The years of neglect not only caused her mental, emotional, and physical torment, but now she was fighting off feelings of ramming scissors through my chest while I slept. Before allowing herself to go crazy or hurt me, she left. A woman who would give her last breath to me if I needed it, who took delight in cooking for me and making sure that I never had to doubt her love and loyalty, walked out the door.

CHAPTER 34

SHE'S NOT HERE

What I assumed would be a brief separation turned out to be far longer and more serious than I ever imagined. Several days went by and I had heard nothing from Carolyn. No phone calls. No text messages. Nothing. Silence from a woman who normally got upset with the news I may have to be away from her for one day.

I was used to getting multiple text messages a day, messages that I sometimes pretended never arrived, especially when she was asking where I was or urging me to call her. Now I only received messages from other women. When Carolyn and I finally did talk, she was curt, and she told me to move on.

Fear shot through my heart as I listened not only to the words, but to the tone of her voice. There was no longer the hint of uncertainty or reluctance from a woman who was hoping to scare me into changing. Instead, I heard a woman too tired to fight for my heart anymore, too tired to wait for me to change. Based on a vision from the Lord, she still maintained that I would change. But the vision did not include her, so she wished me the best with whomever the new woman might be.

A transition took place. Now I was the one asking if there was another man. No longer was I talking to her as an annoyed and indifferent man, but as an attentive and concerned husband. Each day and week that went by only enforced the reality of our trading places. I was the one who now felt abandoned, the one who was calling only to get voice mail. And now I was the one who was feeling sick and tortured over the prospect of another man getting too close or touching what was mine. When she did call, I would get so excited to see her name displayed on my phone. I hoped she was having a change of heart, but her intentions were only to ask about Antwaun Jr. or to inform me how Chante' was doing.

After a considerable time and persistent begging, she agreed to meet me at a nearby store. I did my best to look and smell as good as possible, hoping to resurrect her heart and desire for me again, before the nerve-racking drive to our meeting spot.

The moment I saw her, my heart both jumped and ached. She looked as beautiful as ever, but I also noticed a change in heart and appearance. Her hair was short and in a different style. The happiness that I felt just by having her in my presence helped suppress the misery of what I sensed to be going on in her life.

Her eyes and the familiar smell of her perfume blew me away. I was more than ready to do whatever possible to prove to her I would change. We talked, but I didn't like what I heard or saw from her. No matter how I used my charm, no matter how much I promised her that things would be different, she would only reply calmly, "I'm sorry, Antwaun. It's over, and I've moved on."

I sobbed uncontrollably, asking her why she was doing this to us. I reminded her how she made me promise to never leave her for another, but now she was giving up on me. I was so desperate as she tried to leave that I lay flat on the parking lot, holding her ankles, begging her not to leave. I kissed the top of each shoe as I held on, like I was pleading for my life. As I lay there and looked up, she stared at me like a homeless man who she desperately wanted to help but couldn't. She looked as if to say, "The woman that you are looking for is not here. She's gone."

> **I KISSED THE TOP OF EACH SHOE AS I HELD ON, PLEADING FOR MY LIFE. AS I LAY THERE AND LOOKED UP, SHE STARED AT ME LIKE A HOMELESS MAN THAT SHE DESPERATELY WANTED TO HELP BUT COULDN'T. SHE LOOKED AS IF TO SAY, "THE WOMAN YOU ARE LOOKING FOR IS NOT HERE. SHE'S GONE."**

CHAPTER 35

LOVE LIFTED ME

After seeing Carolyn that weekend, I returned to my scheduled shift as an educator at the prison for juveniles. I walked in smiling, but I was a seriously depressed man. My body was there, but my heart and mind were gone. I just couldn't stop thinking about how hopeless it seemed that I would never again hold Carolyn as my wife. How long would this nightmare last? Was this the unnecessary fate of my marriage?

These consuming thoughts made teaching unbearable. One day, I asked to be relieved when it was evident I was too emotionally unstable and unprepared to handle the typical abuse of a juvenile prison. A prison with verbally and physically aggressive juveniles was not the place to be emotional and distracted. A bad day in the detention center could get you hurt, so removing myself temporarily was the only wise thing to do.

I had worked at the facility for years. I had been in mini riots and other stressful situations, but never had I felt like this. The despair in my heart was too much to keep inside. My soul ached as I tried to cope with the withdrawal of Carolyn's absence. I felt as if she had died and left me alone in a cold world. Every working day became a challenge for me to keep my composure and my sanity.

Thoughts of the way she used to smile at me and even the things that got on my nerves haunted me. As I tasted the hurt, I finally understood the depth of the suffering and agony she had endured. It hadn't even been six months, and I felt like I was going crazy. I couldn't fathom feelings like these for the last seven years she had suffered on and off in our marriage.

It had to have been only God's grace and mercy that kept and sustained her, because only God could give me the strength to make it, not just one day, but one second at a time. The freedom to go out or hook up with another woman was of no interest to me. There was no place I could go, nor any person who I could hang out with who could bring the comfort that I longed for.

Even though Carolyn gave me permission to move on and "do me," I couldn't, nor did I think I would ever get that free agent status from God to give up and move on. I tried, but I kept running into signs that God was not finished with me or my marriage, even after all the dirt I had done.

I TRIED, BUT I KEPT RUNNING INTO SIGNS THAT GOD WAS NOT FINISHED WITH ME OR MY MARRIAGE, EVEN AFTER ALL THE DIRT I HAD DONE.

One sign was from a man who was now divorced himself, but still challenged me to believe that all things were possible with God. I knew that my decision to not give up would really imply if I genuinely believed that. The other sign came from a lady who first tried to convince me to give up hope on my marriage and hinted that she and I could be together. Then, as her voice trembled, she told me that during her prayer time, God told her to tell me to keep trying.

Just as significant, her message was a personal and heart revealing moment that set the stage for putting an end to my running. During a conversation with another woman, she asked me two questions. She asked me what I wanted to do the most and what would make me the happiest. Caught off guard by her questions, I paused and closed my eyes as if to run away and hide in a place where I could forever avoid facing the answers.

I put my head down as she continued to wait. The answers were in my heart, but dormant, locked up, held hostage by my struggle, answers I doubted after falling into sin over and over. Answers that didn't match my inexcusable behaviors.

With tears in my eyes, I finally replied, "To preach the Gospel so that souls would be saved, healed and delivered." I figured that this was not the answer that she expected, nor one conducive to building any potential relationship, but it was the truth. This was what I desired more than Carolyn and I getting back together again: to do God's will, to please Him, to feel His presence, and hear Him say, "well done" at the end of my life.

The truth was that I had been a runaway soldier these many years, AWOL, nevertheless, a soldier. I had allowed myself to become severely discouraged and to believe the devil's lies and to forget what manner of man I really was—isolating myself from brothers and sisters in Christ whenever I fell.

Yes, I was a hypocrite! Yes, I wore a mask, masquerading as a player, pretending to be happy when I was really depressed, and acting as though I belonged to the world when, deep in my heart, I knew I didn't. Consequently, this moment of introspection and enlightenment by God caused me to abort the idea of moving on with another woman to start a new life.

Having a woman in my life was not the answer. I could search a lifetime but never find the place, person, or activity that would bring me the peace of mind that I once had. Running away from my heavenly Father was disastrous. Isolation and soaking in the devil's condemnation didn't make me stronger, but weaker. The question was not if God would forgive me of the harm that I had done to my family, others, and myself, but would I finally forgive myself for the things I allowed to happen.

ISOLATION AND SOAKING IN THE DEVIL'S CONDEMNATION DIDN'T MAKE ME STRONGER, BUT WEAKER.

Although still hurting, the day I let go and accepted the unconditional love of the Father by not just repenting and asking for forgiveness, but by receiving it, was the day I breathed again.

Deleting phone numbers and refusing to yield to the temptation of the club unloaded pressure and silenced the voice of a guilty conscience before God. My hope and faith increased, knowing that as I delighted myself in the Lord, He would give me the desires of my heart. Each day that I focused on God more than Carolyn helped me retrieve the strength, healing, and peace that had left me for so long.

God was working in me, both to will and to do His good pleasure, for without Him breaking my stubborn will, I wouldn't have made it out of the nightmare alive. I now wanted the Lord more than life itself. Even if Carolyn never came back, I knew I would be ok.

What a hard way to receive an education. I could have learned by just listening and obeying the voice of the Lord speaking in my heart or through others, without the unnecessary drama. A degree in obedience is much better than the education of rebellion.

Experientially, I was a witness to the power and deceitfulness of sin and the determination of Satan to destroy a life with purpose within. I understood more than ever the warning to guard my heart with all diligence and to be mindful to take heed lest I fall. I understood more than ever that in me, that is my flesh, dwelled no good thing. I realized the danger of saying with prideful overconfidence the words "I'll never..."

Yes, I understood more clearly the Scripture, "For whosoever will save his life shall lose it." (Matthew 16:25 KJV) It was an understanding that I acquired by curiously opening worldly doors that I wish I'd left closed. Tasting the artificial sweetness of the world's pleasures took me down a road I never thought that I would be on, a road that almost destroyed everything good that God gave me.

How many others started in the right place of peace with God, walking the correct road, only be led astray by the lights of a path called pleasure? How many of us forfeit our peace only to carry so much unnecessary pain? I had needlessly clung to all my worldly pleasures, but now I had triumphantly laid them down. In return, I again saw the faithfulness of God the day Carolyn and I were reunited.

As we searched for a new home, I realized a new chapter of our lives was beginning, all by the mercy and grace of God. That chapter would display the power of God to heal two broken hearts though the virtues of true love and forgiveness. We still had to overcome the consequences of the seeds our sins had sown, but God's power and grace provided the strength Carolyn and I needed.

Gone now were the nights of being out in the street and coming in late and the fear of Carolyn answering my phone. Gone were the panic attacks, insomnia, and antidepressant medication that only treated my issues without ever getting to the root. Dissolved were the fears that I would die without victory over the seemingly unmovable mountain of sexual lust.

A fish is predisposed to survive underwater. A man is not. And no matter how long he may hold his breath, he will soon have to come up for air, because he doesn't belong to that environment.

A FISH IS PREDISPOSED TO SURVIVE UNDERWATER. A MAN IS NOT. AND NO MATTER HOW LONG HE MAY HOLD HIS BREATH, HE WILL SOON HAVE TO COME UP FOR AIR, BECAUSE HE DOESN'T BELONG TO THAT ENVIRONMENT.

In like manner, neither do I belong to this world nor am I able to survive in its corrupt atmosphere apart from my Creator. For it was in Him I was supposed to live, move, and have my being. Holding my breath for so long outside of the atmosphere that I belonged to almost caused me to pass out for life, had it not been for the Lord lifting me out of deep waters...

Whew!!... Yes, that's the sound... When a Man Exhales.

The End.

Bibliography

i   "Praise You In This Storm" (Mark Hall, Bernie Herms) © 2005 Be Essential Songs (BMI) (EssentialMusicPublishing.com) / My Refuge Music (BMI) (CapitolCMGPublishing.com); Banahama Tunes / Word Music LLC (ASCAP) (admin. by WB Music Corp.)

ii   "God Will Take Care of You," 1904, Civilla D. Martin, Public Domain.

iii   "Casanova Brown," Recorded 1983, Epic, Track 1 on Mary C Brockert's, Robbery, ©Sony/ATV Music Publishing LLC, 1983.

iv   "Masquerade," Recorded 1976, Warner Bros, Track 2 on George Benson's Breezin', © Tommy LiPuma, 1976.

v   "Give Me You," Recorded 1987, Qwest Records, Warner Bros. Track 8 on The Winans Decisions, © Marvin Winans, Quincy Jones, Barry Hankerson, 1987.

vi   "Inner City Blues (Make Me Wanna Holler)," Recorded 1971, Hitsville USA, Side 2, Track 3, on Marvin Gaye's album What's Going On, © Marvin Gaye, 1971.

When a Man Exhales!

Thank you for taking the time to read When a Man Exhales. We hope that it helps you realize that when you are faced with life's challenges, you can overcome obstacles as well.

Antwaun is a speaker, author, coach, mentor, youth advocate, and soldier for Jesus Christ. His passion is to warn, inspire and challenge others to live out their purpose, to create meaningful change in his community, to shape the leaders of tomorrow, and to lead by example.

To find out more or book a speaking engagement, please visit AntwaunGay.com.

PRAY ON SOLDIER,

Antwaun Gay

"DETERMINE THAT YOUR FUTURE WON'T LOOK LIKE YOUR PAST."
– ANTWAUN GAY

Made in the USA
Middletown, DE
30 May 2024